COLLECTED POEMS
OF
ELIZABETH BREWSTER

2

We acknowledge the support of the Canada Council for the Arts, the Ontario Arts Council, the Government of Ontario through the Ontario Media Development Corporation's Book Publishing Tax Credit program and the Government of Canada through the Book Publishing Industry Development Program for our publishing activities.

ISBN 0 7780 1246 8 (hardcover)
ISBN 0 7780 1247 6 (softcover)

Cover art by Egon Schiele
Book design by Michael Macklem

Printed in Canada

PUBLISHED IN CANADA BY OBERON PRESS

For Robert Gibbs

In Search of Eros

Sometimes I Think of Moving

IN SEARCH OF EROS

I: The Magic Rod

FOR P.K.P.

I

Do you think
there are interconnections
rhymes rhythms recurrences
that people form a pattern

Do you think there are echoes
that whispers reverberate

Do you think destiny holds us
like wool in her fingers
weaving us in and out?

When we are as far as
sea from prairie
the weaving fingers
tighten the wool.

8

II

Child on the seashore
digging moist sand
into a bucket
playing with pebbles
playing with water
feels all the tides
of all the oceans
rise in her veins
is herself
is I
is you
is everyone
is nobody.

III

In a grain of sand
in a snowflake
there are patterns.
A dreamer drew
the Holy Ghost in the form of a spiral,
and the Milky Way
is also a spiral.

IV

In and out
in and out
we move as in a dance
an elaborate ballet
though I am clumsy
spoil the pattern

except in dreams, where I move
as you move
perfectly
your double
the perfect ballerina

V

And the others move
swans, witches, the prince,
choric observers,
we all move
nobody first
all equal
reflecting one another

moved by the tide
the dance
the snowstorm
the expanding spiral

SPEAK TO ME

Love, speak to me
in the language of birds
their incoherent cries

speak to me
in the language of snakes
uncoiling silently

speak to me
in the language of soft furry animals

speak to me
in the language of fishes
swimming dark pools

Love, speak to me
in the language of men

11

PROPHETESS

I came before, oracle,
but only to the edge of the cave.
I was afraid to go in
and you were sleeping too deeply
for my voice to bring you out.

But now I am ready.
Now I will sink down
into that darkness,
drown if necessary in the wells
of your quicksand eyes.

Speak, sibyl, with your high
ancient voice,
the twittering
of dead swallows;

speak rhymes and riddles
and cracked wisdom;
tell me the world's fortune;
tell me my own fate;
tell me your most true,
most beautiful lies.

12

CONSULTING THE I CHING

I (HEXAGRAM 48: CHING; WELLS)

I am consulting the I Ching
with six pennies, four dimes,
and (since I am short of silver)
two Toronto subway tokens.

The hexagram I am guided to
is for Ching; Wells.

The well is muddy:
it has been forsaken
by men and birds.

Water seeps away from the well
and is wasted.
(The subject of this line of the hexagram
has no one to cooperate above him.)

The well has been cleared out,
but is not used.
"If the king were intelligent,
both he and we
might receive the benefit of it."

The lining of the well
has been skilfully laid.

The fifth line of the hexagram
(which is the most important)
shows a clear well
of sparkling water
from which the traveller drinks
and refreshes himself.

The sixth line shows
the water brought to the top of the well,
standing uncovered.
This line suggests sincerity.

"There will be great good fortune."

II (HEXAGRAM 46: SHENG; ADVANCE)

The subject of the hexagram
advances upward
with the welcome of those above him.

The subject offers
the vernal sacrifices.

The subject ascends
into an empty city.

The subject is employed by the king
to present his offerings.

The subject makes no errors.
He therefore enjoys good fortune.

The subject advances upward
blindly

to the most dangerous place.

III (HEXAGRAM 54: KUEI MEI; GOING HOME)

The hexagram denotes
the marriage of the younger sister
in the position of handmaid
to the true wife.

She delays
she puts off the time
but it will come.

The sleeves of the princess
are not equal to those
of her younger sister.

The moon is almost full.

By the marriage of a younger sister
is suggested
the relation between heaven and earth
which is the source of fruitfulness.

"Any action will be evil."
"There will be good fortune."

15

THE MAGIC ROD

The magic rod
divides the waters
opens a way through the waves.

The magic rod
planted in the ground
becomes a tree.

The magic rod
brings plagues
is awe-full
is fear
is death.

The magic rod
heals all hurt
is blossoming
fragrance
is life.

16

POEM FOR AN AUDIENCE OF ONE

Why do you write?
someone has asked me.
Is it for fame or fortune?
Do you wish to communicate
to a larger audience?
Have you an important message?

I would like to say,
though I don't,
that I write for none of these reasons.

I am writing now
to pass the time
while I am waiting
for you to telephone.

17

POEMS FOR YOUR HANDS

I

Your hand, which has written these poems
that I read in the spring evening,
has also traced poems on my flesh.
The inside of my mouth
has flowered into lyrics;
my breasts are rhymed
couplets;
my belly is smoothed to a sonnet;
and the cave of my body
is a found poem.

II

You say you are an old man
un viellard
and I remember you middle-aged when I was young
yet I feel a wistful youthfulness in you
the unquenched spirit
still flaming in spite of time and wrinkles.

Desire is sad
across this gulf of time.

But touch me lightly
touch my tongue with yours.

Perhaps I could not have stood
the total blaze
of your youth and strength.

III

You disarrange my life.
I cannot predict you.
Saying that you do not know me,
I mean that I do not know you.
I know I could not live with you,
but am frightened also
that I may find it hard to live
without you.

IV

I try to find out facts
about you, so as to feel safe with you.
I want to know all about your brothers
and what games you played as a child
and whether you were unhappy
and if you are afraid of anything.
All this I shall put together;
I shall make a file on you.

In return, I am willing to let you know
that I am afraid of bridges
and of strangers.

V

Without my glasses on
I cannot see you
am only aware of
arms, legs, a head,
the feel of skin
and hair.

You might be God
or my father
or someone I loved when I was young
who is now dead.

You might be a king
or an astronaut.

You might be an oak.

VI

"These are the sort of kisses
Catullus meant," you say.

I wonder if Lesbia ever
wrote any poems.
What a pity
no archaeologist has ever found them.

VII

Let us not be
exclusively solemn.
In spite of the theory
that lust is a serious passion,
there is time even in bed
for a little light
verse.

VIII

"The body knows its mate,"
you say truly
and yet we have our minor difficulties.

But anyhow you tell me
"Next time I'll bring a sign saying
We shall overcome."

IX

You telephone me from your office
where I feel you are bored.

I too have been bored
spring feverish
but I do not say so.

The inconvenience of joy
is that it is habit forming.

X

A pigeon walks along
my window sill
to prove that spring is here.

I do not need his proof
now that I am able to imagine
that we are both young again.

SLOW MOTION

We make love in the afternoon
with the curtains closed.
Cars drive past the window.
A car door slams below us.
Someone is walking down the hotel corridor
knocking on doorways.
We hold our breath till whoever it is goes past.
Your hand rests motionless
on my bare shoulder.
I trace with one finger
the curve of your left eyebrow.

TONGUE-TIED

When we are both dressed
I feel shy with you.
In the restaurant
I look across the table at you
and admire
this distinguished stranger,
as I admire you sometimes
when I see you in a room full of people
talking to someone else.

I feel obliged to make small talk to you
and I forget all the questions
I wanted to ask
and the profound and beautiful things
I would say if I were not tongue-tied.

I am only comforted thinking
that some time again
we shall be naked together.

TIME MACHINE

You tell me that doctors in
the Neurological Institute
can give a signal to the brain
and bring back lost time,
a whole day's sights, sounds, tastes, touches,
all its joys and tedium mixed
real as it was lived.

And I wonder if twenty years from now
I may want to bring back this day,
the hot moist afternoon,
the sound of traffic
outside the open window,
the feel of naked bodies
twined together,
the absurd bed creaking
beneath our weight

even the sense of sadness
when you leave too soon.

GIFTS

I know what you give me, but am not sure
what I give you. Is it just this
pleasure of touch and strangeness?
Are you aware
of my thoughts floating behind my eyes?

When you first touched me
it was the hopeless loves of my youth I thought of;
but now it is you yourself diving
into my depths, swimming
beside me, along my shores. Oh, love,
can I give you anything
so sweet and piercing as this pain?

CHILL

Like all the women who sleep alone
in Chinese poems,
I shiver with the cold.

I would rather have you to warm me
than either a blanket or a poem,
but what can I do?
I pull both poem and blanket
over me now
but neither of them breathes.

ON IMPERMANENCE

Knowing that I cannot say
I will love you forever
or even perhaps for a very long time,
because time itself is against my loving,
and space,
and the sweep and tide of life,
and the restlessness of your will

(yes, and my will, which fears
the danger of love,
its power to hurt)

yet nevertheless I wish I could say it,
and wish to deny
that what is impermanent
is therefore of no importance.

A little longer
I hold your hands in my mind,
and some loneliness in you
which I could not touch,
and the wrong side of your face,
which you did not want me to see;

and I want so much to reach you
across time and space,
to lay my hand on yours,
that it almost seems I might,
and that I might love you,
after all, a little longer.

NURSERY RHYME

My love was past noon
when I was young,
but his heart was light
and his arms were strong.

He was clever,
he was witty,
liked the girls
when they were pretty,

loved to make love,
and knew how too.
Without my love
what shall I do?

EMPTY-HANDED

What can we do for one another?
I see that you are afraid of age and death,
and I am afraid of life without tenderness.
Can I give you youth? Can you give me love?

What is there to do,
but hold each other's hands in pity
and sit on this dark shore waiting
for the tides to wash over us?

WHEN SEA BIRDS CRY

When sea birds cry above the prairie,
when salt winds wash the open plain,
when icebergs melt in the depths of winter
I'll dream I see my love again.

I'll dream your mouth is on my mouth, love;
I'll dream your hand upon my breast.
I'll dream the night is long as winter
when in your arms I find my rest.

GREETING

I walked this morning alone
through the bright white streets
past the white curve of the river.
It was Christmas morning.
Almost nobody was walking.
A man I did not know
called out to me, "Merry Christmas."
I saw his breath steaming
in the blue air.
Answering his words, I wondered
if you were maybe
thinking of me.

YEAR'S END

Unbelievable this whiteness
new as spring blossoms,
all the trees covered with it
and fine drops of it falling
down from strung wire
and all the flat roof of
the newspaper office down below
bright with it.
Airy and white
trees cluster around spires;
smokestacks breathe white,
white clouds float
in the pale sky.

How suddenly this city
which seemed ugly
rises dazzling
as a once-plain woman glowing
beautifully
in the naked eye of the
long-awaited lover.

SUMMER EVENING LIGHTNING

At one time I would have drawn the curtains
to keep out this lightning storm,
but I remember you said
that you liked lightning
and wanted, when you died, to be struck by a thunderbolt—
so godlike a way of being transported.

So I watch the eerie sky,
its blackness
lit by the sudden gleam, the sharp daggers.
I see the church tower upright against the glare,
a stage castle in the midst of shellfire.
A double flame, like a pair of compasses,
squeezes itself shut above the tower.

You walk in my mind,
a winged superman,
somewhere above the tower,
your feet scattering sparks,
your hair in flames,
arrows of thunder
quivering in your hand.

29

II: In Search of Eros

THE PRINCE WHO MARRIED
THE SLEEPING BEAUTY

I thought I had accomplished an adventure
to have chopped my way through the trees
that had grown up
around the sleeping palace,
to have pushed through the stiff,
almost unyielding door
into the passageway.

It was a country summer palace
like an overgrown farmhouse,
Victorian as carved fruit,
full of bric-a-brac and dozing parrots.
In the dusty afternoon
her father snoozed in his stuffed chair,
his beard still growing;
her mother's knitting
fell over the folds of her black bombazine
full-skirted afternoon gown.
They must have expected callers.

Upstairs, the princess
lay on her bed, as pink and beautiful
as previously reported.
She had been reading
a novel from the circulating library,
full of Lady Gertrude and Sir Hugh
and a poet and a governess
and a chimney sweep who was a long-lost heir.
The book was still open at page two hundred.

I awakened her
to a thoroughly satisfactory surprise.
She thought I was Sir Hugh
or perhaps the poet.
Later we became better acquainted.

For a few months after the wedding
we were happy.
Now I am not so sure.
She is still beautiful,
but I find she thinks my parents
are full of crazy modern ideas,
and sometimes she seems happier
talking to my grandfather
than when she is with me.

I've never been able to get her to give up
those whalebone corsets she still fancies.

THE PRINCESS ADDRESSES THE FROG PRINCE

Oh, Frog Prince, Frog Prince,
it was not for you
that I dropped my golden ball
down into the deep water.

It was only by chance
that I dropped it at all.
I intended to stand still
holding the ball safe in my hand
and to look at myself reflected
with my gold crown on my hair
in the pond's surface.

Never in all the stories
was there a more beautiful princess.

And when the ball slipped
and fell from my hand
among the water lilies,
if I expected anyone to rise
from beneath the water

it was a merman or a drowned prince
who would be brought to life
by my eyes.

Never mind, you have a fine voice.
I will take you out of the water
to play in my garden.
I will even take you into the palace.
You shall sit by my gold plate
at dinner time
and be my ugly pet
and sing me songs.

THE BOY WHO MARRIED THE FROG PRINCESS

My eldest brother shot an arrow
into the heart of the town.
The girl who picked it up
was a fine lady.
My second brother shot an arrow
over the land.
The girl who picked it up
was a farmer's daughter.

One wife wore a gold gown
and smelled of musk.
One wife wore homespun
and smelled of hay and apples.

I too shot an arrow,
but I was the family fool,
and only a frog in the pond
swam to me with my arrow.
"Woe's me," I said,
"for I must marry a frog,
and how my brothers will laugh
when they come to visit me."

My two brothers' wives
wove cloth for their wedding sheets.
The farm girl wove coarse canvas.
The lady wove a cobweb
too frail to last,
but my frog wife wove sheets
strong as reed grass,
delicate as dragonfly wings,
to wrap us snug.

My two brothers' wives
baked bread on baking day.
One baked it sour,
the other heavy.
But oh, my little frog wife,
she baked a loaf as light
as a water lily petal,
and honey sweet.

And my brothers' wives said,
"Let us have a great party.
The one of us who dances best
Shall be queen of us all."
The lady could dance a minuet,
the farm girl could square-dance,
but how could my poor little frog wife dance?

My eldest brother's wife
wore star-shaped earrings;
my second brother's wife
wore daisies in her hair.
But my own little wife
wore scarves of lake water.
She danced like ripples,
she danced like foam.

She was land and wave,
she was girl and mermaid.
When I kissed her mouth
she was queen of us all.

34

CINDERELLA

How many girls, washing the supper dishes,
have dreamed this dream:
the great ballroom lit with flaring torches;
velvet and satin crowds
and breasts of diamond,
the stylized ritual of the mating dance;
and underneath the jewelled candelabra
the prince entering
to leap higher than the other males
hold the heroine whirling
in the palm of one hand,
create her beauty
so that in the softened light
she glows a flame or flower.

Afterwards she runs through the garden
barefoot
her single slipper in her hand
her hair down her shoulders;
and, because she forgot time in the prince's arms,
must count time in the passage of long days.

But at length (in the fairy tale)
the prince comes to the door
holding the slipper
in his hand; and only the foot
of the girl washing dishes
will fit the shoe.
          Prince and princess
dance through the wet garden
under the trees of summer,
and all the ice has gone out of the river.

PRINCESS OF EGYPT

The princess, walking by the shore,
found the abandoned child
nested in grasses like a bird.
She clapped her hands and smiled.

Her fans, her slaves, her peacock plumes,
her dark Egyptian face
hovered above the baby's head.
She took him to her breast.

Her plaything and her almost son,
he grew up strong and tall.
She gave him jewels for his ears
and a toy golden ball.

Almost Egyptian, almost prince,
he danced, he rode, he sang.
The golden princess smiled to see
that he was growing man.

Lady, when Moses was full-grown
did he abandon you?
Or did you die before that time?
I hope you did not know

what troubles from your kindness came.
I hope that you died young
and had no other first-born
than this one that you found.

THE GIANT'S HEART

Find where the giant's heart is.
Then you will have
power over his life.

He has planted a tree in an orchard.
On the tree is a gold apple
and in the apple are seeds
and in one of the seeds is the heart
of the great giant.

Or the giant has set his heart
in a gold ring.
You might mistake it for a red ruby,
but it is really his heart.

Or the giant has taken his heart out
and placed it in the body
of this beautiful lady.
See—she has two hearts.

It is foolish of the giant
to keep his heart out of his body
in ring or apple or lady,
in mine or well or cave

but heroes must always take advantage
of the foolishness of giants
and try not to be like them.

KIND AND UNKIND

Once upon a distant time
when the gods rewarded good,
a mother and two daughters lived
in a farmhouse near a wood.

Small was the house, the fields were small,
with a small barn and a small stable,
some hens, a horse, a cow, that gave
the milk and butter for the table.

Now if the mother had been wise
they might have lived together well,
busy and happy all the year,
with food to eat and some to sell.

But she so favoured Gwendolyn,
her elder, stupid, lazy daughter,
Elsie, the younger, worked alone,
and milked the cows, and carried water.

Elsie was both good and gay,
kind to the poor, the old, the weak,
and beautiful as she was kind,
with golden hair and rosy cheek.

(No wonder Gwendolyn disliked her.
I fear I might have loathed her too
if I had a younger sister:
alas, dear Reader, so might you.)

From the wood a friendly witch
came to watch these sisters work,
saw how Elsie slaved all day,
how her sister used to shirk.

One day, then, the witch approached,
dressed in ancient skirt and veil,
sat beside the well where Elsie
came to fill her water pail.

"Prithee, girl," the witch demanded
(she had read an older tale)
"Give me water. I am weary
and my strength and courage fail."

Elsie gave her water then,
brought her bread and country cheese,
helped her find her pathway home,
chatted to her at her ease.

Homeward then she took her way
to the farmhouse where her mother
and her sister waited for her,
grumbling of her to each other.

"Why," the angry mother asked,
"Did you wander to the wood
while the chores were to be done?
I'll be bound you sought no good."

Elsie opened up her lips,
but from her mouth when she would speak
roses mixed with rubies fell,
the garden blossomed at her feet.

"Gwendolyn," the mother said,
"You too must seek to win your fortune.
Diamonds and wheat may be your gift
if fairies give you too a portion."

So Gwendolyn, that idle girl,
went grumbling off with swinging pail
and found again the ancient woman,
with ragged cloak and dusty veil.

"A gift, fair girl," the old witch said.
"Give me a drink of good well water.
I'm tired, I'm lost, my legs are sore:
help me, as you would help your mother."

"I have no time to waste on you,"
Gwendolyn said, the rude and greedy.
"I came in search of fairy gifts,
and not to help the old and needy."

The witch then flung aside her veil.
She was as grand as any queen,
and tall, and young, and proud, and straight,
she stood and stared down Gwendolyn.

"Girl," she said, "who would not give
to the poor and weak and old
even a single kindly word,
you too will suffer age and cold;

suffer from unkindness too,
bitter thoughts and bitter words.
If you have children they will cut
your heart to bits with swords."

40

Frightened, Gwendolyn rushed home,
screaming loudly as she ran,
and with every scream there fell
a toad or frog to ground.

Sad that toads and frogs should creep
where her sister's roses grow
and where Elsie's rubies lie
Gwendolyn's worms and spiders go.

Moral

Who speaks kind words speaks roses, say
white witches and good godmothers.
Now pity those like Gwendolyn
(or like your Author) who fare worse.

SISTER SELVES

In real life
the kind and unkind sisters
are usually the same person.
Regan-Goneril and Cordelia
share bodies on alternate days,
scold their father and then weep over him.
They are forever poisoning each other
or putting each other into prison.

How can the old king know
when his favourite daughter
will escape from her wicked sister's eyes
and kneel before him?

Toads and roses fall together
from the cruel tender mouth
of the Kind-Unkind,
double gifts
of the godmother witch.

STAGE SETTING

The great grey winged and feathered clouds
sweep over the prairie sky.
Thunder rolls in the distance.
A dog barks in the yard below.

OLD LEAR, THE CRAZY KING

Old Lear, the crazy king,
caught in a storm,
found only a hovel's roof
to keep him warm,
no palace for his bare bones.

Trust not to age or blood,
trust not to riches,
trust not to your body's children
that they will not be bitches
or arrant knaves.

But fools may help you some,
and storms will not deceive you,
and those with harshest tongue
may most relieve you
when you are most in need,
like Lear, the crazy king.

FOOL'S SONG

If chimney pots fall down
and the world is shaken,
what do cats and suns care
if they've no harm taken
when chimney pots fall down?

When cats lie in the sun
and suns lie in the sky,
if chimney pots are shaken
what care I?—
since cats lie in the sun.

43

LEAR

Even Lear
was not too old to learn,
old Lear, the child again,
taught by his wicked daughters;
the fool Lear, taught by his fool;
tempestuous Lear, taught by the tempest;
royal Lear, taught by Poor Tom;
blind Lear, taught by a blind man.

And what did you learn,
when the rain came and your wits turned?
What did you learn, old man?
that the gods are just? or crazy?
that hearts can break at eighty
as well as at eighteen?
that the universe
is no flatterer?
Or did you learn chiefly
the meaning of the word "never"?

Whatever your learning,
it came too late for life.
Whatever your learning,
it could only be of use
as a warning in a tale,
as a halo over your white head
where you stand on the stage forever
holding your beloved dead
in your dying arms.

44

IN SEARCH OF EROS
Selections from a longer poem

I: PSYCHE AND THE LAMP

So, wearied in her mind with questionings,
Tossed between doubt and doubt, wishing to have
Some certain knowledge, be it evil or good,
And troubled even by the side of love,
She lay awake when he seemed fast asleep.
Her heavy eyes, unvisited by sleep,
Searched in the darkness, but could trace no features
In the face beside her, known but never seen.
She knew where the lamp was and where the matches,
And where the knife too that her sisters gave her,
Could find them in the dark; but in her mind
She hunted for them often, often lit
The lamp, often stood poised, the knife
Clasped in her frightened hand, before that hour,
Not able longer to bear doubt, she crept
Out from the bed, and softly tiptoeing,
Half hesitating, half turning back, and then
Stepping with resolution, reached the lamp,
And put her fingers round its glassy base.
And still, she thought, if the voice called out, "Psyche,
Where are you, Psyche?" such grace was in that voice
She would put down the lamp, turn back, and know
She knew his features by its music.

45

Her love was sleeping, though, and no voice spoke.
Here were the matches, waiting by the lamp,
With the knife near them, hidden in a drawer.
Now, when the lamp was lit, shading the flame
To keep from waking those still-drowsy eyes,
Back to the bed she tiptoed, knife in hand,
And bent above the pillow. There she paused
Awhile before she dared to look;
Then, bending down, she saw the handsome boy
Asleep and dreaming, with his head flung back,
One arm still resting in her empty place.
Joy and relief wheeled in her dizzy head.
The treacherous lamp shook in one trembling hand,
While from the other slipped the cruel knife
And woke and wounded love.

II: SHE IS A PILGRIM

Now Psyche as a pilgrim wandered forth
To seek her love.
She must wear out seven pairs of iron shoes
And fill seven vials full of tears before
She found her love again. It was December,
A bitter day, with wind heaping the snow
Into great drifts, in which poor Psyche floundered,
For all the roads were blocked—no snow-ploughs then.
Yet she continued: she was used to snow,
No town-bred girl from the tropics. She'd survive.
So on she struggled, with spruce on either side
Loaded with snow, or sometimes past a farmhouse
With children out in front, playing at snowballs.
The wind died down, and the cold air stood still;
The snow stopped drifting, hardened into crust,
A smooth, hard surface over which she walked
With ease, held up even on iron shoes.

Under the blue, bright sky of the afternoon
The crust shone blue; but when night came it sparkled
Bright as the stars that sparkled over it,
Those small, hard lumps of ice that shine in the sky.
And as she travelled under the eye of the moon
She came in view of a great mountain height.
At first it looked of glass, but was cold ice,
Covered with sprinkled snow. Straight in her road
It lay, and she could see no path around it.
So sheer the ice was that she could not climb it.
She must go back and ask the nearest farmers—
A long way back they lived—another way,
Or give the whole trip up and go back home.

But as she sat in sorrow on the ground,
Bitterly chewing in her mind the crust
Of grief, her wandering eye caught sight
Of a great bird's skeleton, the bones plucked clean,
And "Oh," she thought, "if that bird were alive,
I'd sit on his back, and his great flapping wings
Would lift me past this mountain." Then some voice,
Perhaps the bird's own, whispered her to take
The bones of the skeleton and make a ladder,
And with this ladder climb across the mountain.
And she obeyed, and with laborious steps
Climbed up the mountain and down the other side.

47

A strange and dangerous place that mountain was,
With cliffs and crags of ice, and slopes of ice,
Shining all colours in the light of the moon;
Yet with her ladder she journeyed safe enough
Until she came to near the foot of it,
And then the bones gave out. "What shall I do?"
She thought. "It's still too far to jump."
But then she took the knife out of her pocket,
And cutting off her finger, used that bone
As the last rung of the ladder. Blood ran down
The icy slope, and from the snow there sprang
A rose or two, thinking that June had come.

III: ADVENTURE UNDERGROUND

So Psyche started once more on her travels.
She had not far to go to find the mouth
Of the underworld, for that lies always near,
Though guarded by an iron gate. She knocked
Awhile before the porter came, a man
Forbidding in his look, who opened up
The gate a crack, but did not let her in.
"What is your name?" he asked. "Love's wife, called Psyche,
Sent by my husband's mother for a box
Someone's to give her." Then he let her in,
Barring the gate behind her. "You may wish,"
He said, "you had not come. The way is long
And full of dangers. But that is your affair.
There is the path you follow." This dark path
Led through a twilight landscape, sloping downward,
Where fog crept round her, and she could not see
More than a step ahead at any time.
So down the gradual, perilous descent,
She felt her way, and stumbled
Sometimes on stones half-hidden in the road,
Or felt a bramble catching at her skirt.

48

At a turn in the path, the fog decreased a little,
But then she wished it back, for here she saw
A pack of hungry bears that she must walk through.
She stopped to get her courage up, and they
Advanced to meet her, growling. Almost she
Said farewell to her life, but then she thought
Of her husband, and remembrance of his face
Strengthened her to go on. They stood aside,
Though with a hungry look at her, and she
Went on her way beyond them. No life stirred
For some time on the path. Only dead bracken
Crackled beneath her feet. And then she heard
A noise like steam escaping; wondering,
She approached the noise, and sudden from the ground
A thousand snakes' heads started. Round they coiled
And darted out fierce tongues, wreathing their bodies
In oily convolutions. These frightened her
More than the bears; but them she also passed,
While they upreared themselves to sting, but failed.
                    Beyond the snakes
There was a narrow valley, piled with heaps
Of slimy ordure, giving forth a stench
That almost turned her stomach. Here she might
Have died of suffocation, but pure air
Breathed in upon her when she thought of love.

So down through varied dangers and strange scenes
She made her way, until at last she came
To the door of the dark central chamber, guarded
By all the foes she'd passed before, and more:
Fire-breathing lions, witches with red eyes
Like coals of fire, giants with flaming torches;
But through them all she made her way, and opened
The heavy door, that creaked to let her past.

Inside the dim-lit room, she looked around,
Expecting to find more and still more giants.
But nothing stirred within. The place was empty.
There was no furniture, only bare floors,
And dark, cavernous walls. Then she sat
Down on the damp, cold floor and waited there
Long hours, not knowing what to do,
And in the blankness almost she forgot
Her husband's face, and almost fell asleep.
But still she did not sleep, and finally
She felt a something moving in the room,
A breath of wind, perhaps; it came towards her,
And she half-glimpsed a figure draped in shadows
That bent above her, caught her by the hand,
And pressed within her palm a metal box,
Then vanished. Was the figure real? she wondered.
But the box was real enough. She felt
The carving on its cover. This must be
The box she should take back.
                                    So now, arising,
She made her way back through the sentried door,
Back the long pathway through the snakes and bears,
Through the still-foggy landscape, to the place
Where the porter stood, surprised to see her living.
Yet he said nothing, but unbarred the gate
And let her through once more. And so she came
Up to fresh air and sunlight once again.

PSYCHE AND CUPID

If Psyche had not found
Cupid above or underground;
if all the tasks she ever strove
to do won not his love;
if all the helpers proved untrue,
and angry Venus beat her black and blue;

I wonder then
if Psyche would have sought him still,
or turned to men
less godlike but of easier will?

But luckily
for Psyche and for Cupid too,
he did not try her strength to that degree,
but when she sought him
came to meet her: so
the poets say, and surely they should know.

ROSA

Often as Rosa was in love,
each time she thought it was forever,
for this one had enchanting eyes,
and that one was much more than clever;

and one she liked the way he kissed,
and one the way he never did,
one for Byronic melancholy,
and one for gaiety and wit;

one for his sturdy common sense
and one because he was a fool,
and one whose tantrums all were hot,
and one whose blood was always cool.

Each time she thought it was forever,
and every time her heart was broken,
and yet she woke another day
to see another love awaken.

WILLIE LUMP LUMP

The loneliest man in the world is dead
the newspaper says;
or maybe he was just
the ugliest man in Canada,
with a disease
which made tumours grow
at the nerve ends of his skin,
so that even in penitentiary
people called him Willie Lump Lump.

His family was ashamed of him;
waitresses wouldn't wait on him;
he had no job.
He tried to kill himself three times
but always failed.

But his one friend
a widowed old age pensioner said
"He was a very nice man.
He wanted to work as a night watchman
because of his face, you see."
But now he is dead.

Death is no plastic surgeon
but he does shape new faces
gradually.

PORTRAIT OF A WOMAN WITH PIGEONS

In the Carleton Street graveyard
a fat woman in a fur coat
is feeding pigeons.
She is pulling scraps
from her shopping bag,
and dozens of pigeons
cluster on the snowy ground
or on a park bench
or on one of the tombstones.
One or two squirrels
are hopping towards
the congregation.

Catching sight of me,
she is embarrassed,
caught like a saint or a child
in absurd beneficence.
"Hurry," she calls
to the approaching squirrels.

ROMANCE

Mary tells me she admires the salmon
because it is such a romantic fish.
It travels two thousand miles in order to spawn,
then dies in a ritual of love and death,
its flesh feeding new generations.

But I am relieved to discover
that only Pacific salmon
are in fact so feeble.
Atlantic salmon make the trip to spawn
several times,
though every spawning
leaves another scar
and they are ringed like trees.

55

THREE SONNETS ON *THE SCARLET LETTER*

HESTER PRYNNE

The great red A that frightened children so
burned on her breast. They thought that she was Sin.
Embroidered flame announced the flame within,
blazing on blackness that was deep as woe.

She was like forests that are dark as night,
haunted by witches and by savages,
where fruits and mosses cling to ancient trees
and men are lost and fade away from sight;

or like an ocean into which men fall
and drown themselves within the salty flood.
Over their heads there flowed her tidal swell,
the lunar promptings of her flesh and blood.

Dimmesdale was drowned. Old Roger, on the shore,
Envied his drowning. He could do no more.

ROGER CHILLINGWORTH

Revenge and love, twined in a single strand
like lovers' hair in our grandfathers' days,
wound round his heart and strangled it. His gaze
was like a lover's, which must understand
all motions, probe the depths of the loved eyes
for all past secrets and dead sympathies.

Stealthy and slow, his undiscovered lust
moved sidelong to unbutton Dimmesdale's mind.
He must possess his thoughts; his hands must find
his heart, and feel his agony undressed.

His victory was to know the man had sinned.
But in his conquest he himself was lost
and in his owning he himself was owned.
Dimmesdale possessed him, and the weak had won.

ARTHUR DIMMESDALE

Pride of remorse devoured him day by day.
Not God could pardon, for his guilt was heaped
sky-high. Not tears, but blood, he wept,
poured out to God, his loving enemy.

The anguished copulation of a prayer
could not avail; for surely he had done
an evil act, was worse than others were,
since his unfaithfulness was to the One

and infinite God. This dark adultery
bred falsehood in the mind. It filled his heart
full of a strange and naked blasphemy,
and gave him dreams of terror. Waves of sweat

broke on him. He slept, and dreamed again
of Hester's flesh, that made and marred him man.

ALL'S WELL THAT ENDS WELL

When Helen followed that ungrateful boy,
her husband, from one city to another,
schemed, wheedled, tricked, and used her honest craft
to get him and his ring—was he worth the bother?

How did she like her prize when she got home
with it to Rousillon? Was his curled hair
enough to make her happy, or did she long
for courts to visit and for kings to cure?

Did he flirt with other girls, find her pedantic,
her conversation too medicinal?
Did she freeze his buddies out of the castle gates
or retreat from them into her own still

feminine chamber? Did her mother-in-law
wrangle with her at times? When she was alone
was she sometimes glad Bertrand was out of sight?
And what was breakfast like at Rousillon?

III: Inanna

DEATH OF THE GODS

Who was the last person to say a prayer
to the old gods, to Jupiter or Diana,
Ceres or Venus? And did whoever said it
say it with belief, or only as a sort of charm
half remembered from childhood?
Did someone say to her (I know she was a woman)
"You mean you still believe
all those old stories? All the modern people
have changed over to the new religion.
Nobody in town,
nobody with any education,
would pray now to one of those dusty ancients.
It's not fashionable—
anyhow, it's not even legal."

But somewhere in the country
in a hovel under trees
some old crone dying in her bed
whispered a name she had heard in childhood
to protect her from the dark,
from the shades of the underworld;
and the goddess of hearth or orchard,
of moon or love or wisdom,
or the god of vine or thunder,
or the goatfoot god,
came and took her hand,
descended with her into the shadows,
and (except by the lips of lying poets)
was never called back again.

Could you still be called back,
ancient gods and goddesses?
Or have you slept so long
with no cries from your children
that there will never again be a morning for you?
Deities with so few petitions
might well be the most easily secured,
the best listeners.

Oh seaborn Venus, heavenly Juno,
oh dark Persephone, daughter of the Earth,
from where you rest in the arms of death
I call you.

Dionysus, true Vine,
hand me your chaliced blood.

60

FOR THE UNKNOWN GODDESS

Lady, the unknown goddess,
we have prayed long enough only
to Yahweh the thunder god.

Now we should pray to you again
goddess of a thousand names and faces
Ceres Venus Demeter Isis
Inanna Queen of Heaven
or by whatever name
you would be known

you who sprang from the sea
who are present in the moisture of love
who live in the humming cells
of all life
who are rain
with its million soft fingers

and you who are earth
you with your beautiful ruined face
wrinkled by all
that your children have done to you

sunlike lady
crowned with the whirling planets.

Lady of peace, of good counsel,
of love, of wisdom

we invoke your name
which we no longer know

and pray to you
to restore our humanity
as we restore your divinity.

MOON

Was it not the goddess of the moon
who destroyed Actaeon in her forests?
He came too close to her, he gazed
without protection at her nakedness

She turned him into a wild stag,
and his own hounds
his servants
leaped at his throat and killed him.

Was it not his fault,
the foolish man
who came into the moon's forests,
who climbed the moon's mountain,
who looked too close
at the naked moon?

INANNA

When the goddess Inanna
descends to the underworld

she must take off her crown
and go without pride

she must take off her jewels
and go without adornment

she must take off her clothes
and go without veils.

The queen of the sky
must sink into the ground;
the queen of the sunrise
must swallow darkness;
the queen of life
must remove her gown of flesh
and sleep in dust.

THREE JOYFUL MYSTERIES

Annunciation comes in spring. The snow
is melted to puddles in the sudden sun.
Packs of it slide like thunder from barn roofs,
with icicles turned to water from the eaves.
Over the brown and muddy fields the crows
flap cawing, and the earliest song sparrow
sings love songs to the earth.

And now the Angel, walking through the yard,
moves Mary-ward; in this grey farmhouse
she may be in the kitchen kneading bread
or upstairs making beds, or in the dairy
churning the cream to butter; or she stands
here in the window where the sun pours love.

The earth waits
for the fall of the seed in its furrows,
for sun and rain.
Gently it will protect, with its veins nourish
grass, violets, oats,
the rich and foaming clover.
In time it will be
perpetual mother.
But now it is young and cold from the snow; it turns
awakening
towards the sun and the love song of the bird.

64

It was a summer day that Mary came
to see her cousin, old Elizabeth,
that woman who expected a strange birth,
whose spring had come in winter of her life.
She walked the dusty road into the village
between the hayfields ripening on each side
and all the richness of the summer's green.
She too was a field, she thought, a blossoming tree
whose fruit would ripen slowly in the winter.

Now there were children sitting in the pasture,
deep in the clover and the foaming daisies,
hugging the patch of shade beneath the elm trees,
picking wild strawberries, pulpy and red and sweet.
They called to each other
across a world of green.

Her cousin, watching from the kitchen window,
had seen her coming, and slamming the screen door,
walked out to meet her, moving heavily,
she was so near her time.

BIRTH

The child was born in winter. Deep December
had piled the snow halfway to the barn roof.
The cows and horses huddled in the stable,
warming each other with their friendly breaths.
Under the pines the snow was blue and crusty,
and the white fields stretched cold beneath the stars.

It was a frosty night for love to come
into the world; but love, conceived in spring,
ripened to fullness in the autumn weather,
is born at last in winter, burning son
in the cold stable of our battered hearts.

MAN WITH GOSPEL MESSAGE
(Verbal Transcription)

I (LAZARUS)

When I was young
(the man says)
I died once
for twenty minutes.

My eyes have never seen
so clear again.
I saw inside,
I saw even the springs
inside my mattress.

II (BIBLE)

What is wrong,
he says,
is all the churches.
What is wrong
is the way they worship texts

so that there was this woman
who burned out her eye
so that it would not see evil

and this man
who cut his child's hand off
for stealing honey.

III (GHOSTS)

It is the spirits that do all the harm
(he says).
All the spirits from the past invade you.
There was this girl
a French-Canadian girl
who had her body taken over by the ghost
of a tubercular German immigrant
and found she could only speak German.

Now you can't altogether blame the ghost—
she wanted a life, too, see?—
but it was sure hard on the girl
not to be able to speak
either of the right languages.

IV (CHOSEN PEOPLE)

God speaks to me, too,
and I tell you
he always speaks in English.

Every morning
just before breakfast
he speaks.

I have decided the Anglo-Saxons
are the chosen people.

V (CALL TO ACTION)

I tell you it only needs a few people
to take over any one of these churches,
United Church or whatever.

It only needs a few people
to take over the governments
of countries.

It only needs a few people
to overturn the world.

68

JESUS REVOLUTION HITS ALBERTA
A Group of Found Poems
(from The Way, Vol. 3, No. 2, July 1972)

I

Look
the "unexpected"
is happening again
A special highlight
coming to Calgary.
Spiritual stampede
at Immanuel Assembly
17th Ave & 1st St. S.W. Calgary
Meet the Minneapolis God Squad
July 9—16
26 dynamic youth
who "wowed" thousands
during recent Caribbean tour.

II

I FOUND HAPPINESS

I thank the Lord
for all He's done for me...
saved me at the age of eight...
at the age of 17,
I turned my back on Him
completely, ran wild,
hitchhiked all over the country...
my problem was
I did not fear God....

Then I came to the city of Red Deer
and my ideas about God changed.

I believe
that my testimony is typical....

III

The camp you cannot afford to miss.
FAMILY CAMP Bible Conference.
Please bring all your bedding supplies
(a warm bed roll
or adequate sleeping bag,
pillow, blankets, bed sheets)....
Girls: hot pants and mini skirts
are undesirable dress during camp.

IV

Our family
moved to Alberta in 1969
and I started going to university,
a place which is as close
to HELL on earth
as man has ever been.

V

JESUS T-SHIRTS
in medium and large sizes
are now available....

The following messages
appear on shirt fronts:
    1. God is Love
    2. Jesus Loves You
    3. Jesus is Lord
    4. Praise the Lord
    5. Turn from your sin
       and believe the Good News of Jesus
       or else....

VI

Jesus is where it's at.
Jesus is coming!

THE BLUE PEN

Heaven is not necessarily true
because I would like to believe in it—
No, nor necessarily false either.
How do I know what is or is not,
when I don't even know what is this hand
that holds my blue pen
or what makes the pen blue?
It looks the way it does because of the way
it absorbs or throws off light
or the way light hits my eye,
whatever light is
or whatever my eye is.
The pen's solidity,
like its blueness,
is probably a kind of illusion.

All this time, all this year, spent
talking to students about books,
those solid three dimensional objects,
or reading the words of students
written with their blue pens

And I do not know, do not know,
cannot really tell them,
only know when I disagree with them,
do not know
what is poetry or what is blue
(though I look now at the sky
and see what is blue)
or if God and heaven are myths
(myth being a fancy literary name
for a lie).

I think I would like to turn my life
back to page one and read it all again
so maybe it would make sense
because it seems I am still always
asking the same questions
that I asked myself (and sometimes answered)
when I was ten or twenty,
like Who am I?
and Who are all these others?
Whose novel is it
that we have stumbled into?
Does the author intend
a happy ending or an endless fall
down through light years of space?

Why do I sometimes wake up
during my dreams
convinced the dream is true?

PLAYING INDIAN

Playing Indian in the back orchard
with a feather stuck behind my ear
dropped from one of the moulting hens,
I believed in the existence of Indians
neither more nor less than I believed in Robin Goodfellow
or ghosts or elves.
They were invented, maybe,
by Longfellow or Fenimore Cooper;
on the other hand (like ghosts)
might really be true.

Once an Indian woman came to the door
selling woven baskets
and little bunches of mayflowers.
But the woman looked no different
from any of the neighbour women
with a good tan.
No feathers.

My mother put lemon juice on her face
after being in the sun,
or sometimes cucumber,
to make sure her skin stayed white.
"Why do you want to tan?" she said.
"It makes you look just like an Indian."

Indians, my mother said,
used to live in the woods,
but didn't any longer.
Robin Hood had lived in the woods too,
and so had the Nut Brown Maid.
Now there were only bears and squirrels.
Anyhow I was not to go to the woods.
People got lost there.

It was only in *Hiawatha*
that Indians prayed to the Manitou.
Now they were Christians
the same as everybody else.

TRAPPED

If I were an ant crawling on a blade of grass,
I would be unaware of all those beings
planning to step on me
or to spray me with insecticide.

If I were a giant so large I was invisible,
I would step peacefully from planet to planet
and stride beyond all these troubles.

But I am just the wrong size. I am human.

IV: Pilgrim

ON THE NATURE OF THE HERO

It is always the youngest son or the fool
who accomplishes the adventure,
though he sets out after the others leave.
He is the one who finds the magic well
and brings back the water that will cure his father.
He picks the golden apple from the tree
guarded by the great green dragon.
He kills the giant, steals his moneybags,
and makes off with the giant's daughter
or the princess whom the giant had wickedly kidnapped.

His brothers always laugh at him to begin with,
say he is a child, a mother's pet,
or they plot against him, hide him in a well;
but in the end he has to rescue them,
free them from giants or famine,
share the moneybags, provide them with ladies
not quite so well-born as his princess
but good enough for them.

And it is always the youngest daughter or the ugly one
who is rescued or married by the hero,
changed from her dragon or frog shape by his kiss.
She is the one who makes a long journey
to find her husband or her missing brother,
who guides the hero through a maze of dangers
and when he is dead takes all his scattered bones
and sews them back together,
breathes life into them
so that he wakes again.

It is the youngest son or youngest daughter
who stops to pet the cat, talk to the bear,
share crumbs with birds,
help the lame old woman,
listen to the blind man
telling stories by the kitchen fire.

Are youngest children
really the most kind or the most adventurous?

Or is it the youngest son or the fool
who sings the songs?
Is it the youngest daughter or the ugly one
who tells the stories?

77

MY UNKIND SELF

Why do I feel guilty towards the old woman
who lives next door,
who brings me date squares and fancy cakes
and wants to talk to me?

She asks me questions,
but is too deaf to hear
any of my answers.

I think she has invented a whole
life for me.
She has decided that I am a nurse,
married, but separated from my husband,
and she supposes that I have a daughter
living somewhere with my parents.
She is sorry for me,
and thinks I need to be fattened up,
though I tell her desperately that I am overweight,
and would like to tell her that I don't like cake.

Should I bake cookies just to take her some?
Should I ask her about her grandchildren?
(But she can't hear me.)

I am afraid my face shows
that I am not interested.
I am afraid that if she were a white witch
she would never be tempted to give me my three wishes.
If I were younger, I could pretend
that I would never live to be so old.

MARVEL

What magic caves and orchards
could have held more marvels
than the child's real world?
The black cat suckling her kittens
at small pink breasts;
the eggs, still warm from the cackling hen,
brought in from the straw-smelling henhouse;
ants in the barnyard,
marching in columns, carrying small bundles,
under the tall sunflowers;
the dust in a column of sunshine;
your own shadow, growing or diminishing.

Or even toys, a horseshoe-shaped magnet,
or the wooden blocks with which you built castles,
or the fat wooden man who stood up again
when you knocked him down,
or the inherited glass fire engine,
or the paper dolls cut from Eaton's catalogue,
or the swing under the trees
where you flung yourself at the sky.

And marvellously, as with a charm
(like the one you said rubbing your baby warts
with a cut potato),
they have all disappeared.

Paper dolls burned;
blocks, toys become rubbish;
the cat, hens, ants, sunflowers
long ago dead;
the dust reconstituted
to other dust.

Even the shadow the child cast
is not the same shadow.

MIRRORS

Mirrors are always magical.
So the child knows
who first sees one: the strange object
in which the other little girl appears
wearing the same dress, encircled in the same arms;
smiles, frowns, looks puzzled, cries, all the same
but somehow different.
For the other child does not have flesh, feels shiny to touch
and cold like the mirror's surface.

Mirrors are magic, and behind their surface
surely there is another Alice world
where you can walk and talk.

Mirrors are solid lakes,
and you could drown
beneath them if their outer layer cracked,
spin down and meet your real self far below,
a mermaid princess combing out your hair
before a magic mirror.

NIGHT AIR

"Come in, come in out of the night air," my aunt called.
"You shouldn't be outdoors in the night air."
And she summoned us in
from the sweet, dangerous, witching breath
of the evening-fragrant flowers.

Sweet, hot, and damp the air was.
We had played hopscotch in the liquid dusk.
I had just learned three new words:
twilight, honeysuckle, whippoorwill.
Now that night had come
there was no telling when it would be over.

PASTORAL TRADITION

Reading *As You Like It* reminds me
how I read it as a child, and thought
it could take place in the bush somewhere
beyond the cow pasture
where there were deer and chipmunks
and the fern-tasting blueberries grew.

But Orlando never came wandering
past with poems to stick on trees,
and I never saw Rosalind sitting
on the log fence of the pasture
making witty conversation
with melancholy Jaques.
There were no dukes eating picnic lunches,
or courtiers to sing to them,
and not even Touchstone
on a day's jaunt from the city
gingerly avoiding the
dried pats of cowdung.

But "What is poetical?" Audrey asked.
"Is it honest?"
                    Touchstone said no.

THE SIEGE OF TROY

Meanwhile, while Troy was being besieged,
life went on in Ithaca as usual.
Penelope did her weaving.
Telemachus was growing up.

All through my childhood
Hitler goose-stepped on the front page,
Mussolini spoke to crowds from balconies.
My cousins and I made mudpies,
played "London Bridge is Falling Down,"
worried about other things
than Spain and Ethiopia.

I grew up. I went to classes
in a quiet town by a river
while London was being blitzed
and bombs dropped on Hamburg;
and what I remember about D-day
is having tea with lettuce sandwiches.

No doubt the day of Waterloo
there were births and marriages
as well as deaths.
No doubt on Judgment Day
there will be someone out selling hot dogs,
and children will cool themselves
with ice-cream cones.

THE RETURN OF HOMER

Weep for Troy in flames
after all these centuries.
Again the palaces
slums and highrises
crumble with the heat.

Again we have carried
with our own hands
destruction into our city.

We shall become once more a story
mostly false
of heroes and beauty
praised by the blind.

Some day our city
will again be excavated
if there are any hands to excavate
these ashes, these broken dishes,
these heaps of
garbage, bones, used cars,
old tin cans, plastic,
this discarded
universe.

GOLDEN WEST

Disembarking from our aircraft at the city,
we were met by men and women dressed to kill
in sombreros, fancy waistcoats, and cowboy boots.
"Welcome," they cried heartily.
"Welcome to our city,
the Gateway to the Golden West."
They greeted us with badges and handshakes.
Some of them even embraced us,
while children handed us folders,
and a band played stridently
in the background.

We pushed our way through the packed airport
looking for someone who looked to be waiting for us,
but the man who was supposed to meet us
was not there,
and when one of us tried to telephone him
the operator said there was no such person.

We lugged our heavy bags
out to the sidewalk
and waited for our unknown taxi driver.

ALDEN NOWLAN IN THE
WINNIPEG AIR TERMINAL

I kept intending to write a poem
about Alden Nowlan writing a poem
in the Winnipeg air terminal;
but he was always escaping,
flying off to a telephone booth,
zooming over the telegraph wires
        like Icarus
to some fantastic country,
while I was still sitting
in the Winnipeg air terminal
beside a potted palm
trying to draw a picture
of a heavy bearded man
        writing
with a ballpoint pen
in his little black notebook
        and stopping now and then
to draw funny pictures.

86

POEM FOR AL PURDY

Reading a note about you,
I suddenly realize why you always seem familiar
when I see you at poetry readings.
Your birthday, I read, is December 30.
You share the same birthday with my father
and my eldest brother.
So I grew up with the voices of those Capricorns,
the long loping sentences, the easy gestures,
the anecdotes going on forever
with my non-talkative mother sometimes trying to halt them;
my brother drunk and singing all night
his parodies of Baptist hymns;
my father clowning
with some story about his days in the army
           ("So he says to me, Sarge...")
and suddenly in the midst of clowning sad,
sad to tears as my mother never was.

And I, not born under Capricorn,
never able to tell a funny story
all the way through
without breaking down somewhere in the middle,
I don't know you, mightn't like you if I did
(don't often write letters to my brother)
but nevertheless I play over a record of your poetry
to hear again what seems a family voice.

POEM FOR A YOUNG SORCERESS

The witch is young.
Her uncoiled hair
slides down her back.
Her gaze is clear,

her forehead smooth,
her smile discreet,
her manner guarded,
distant-sweet.

The spirit who
obeys her spell
I think is tricky
Ariel.

She reads my palm
my horoscope.
I listen with
half-mocking hope,

but wonder
what her fate will be
who smiles and tells
my fate to me.

39 NORTH CASTLE STREET, EDINBURGH, 1820

Almost I can see the room, almost:
the drawing room lit by one large gas lamp,
the Chinese wall paper, the pianoforte,
the silver tea service,
a green Empire sofa by the wall.

The gentlemen have come from the dining room
not drunk but jovial
after their claret.
They talk well.
They sit with the ladies and sip bohea
recovering from their argument about politics.

Sir Walter's wife wears red feathers
and too much rouge.
One pretty daughter, dressed in white,
is playing
the fashionable harp.
The other sings.

At ten exactly
(since they were up at dawn)
they will light tapers
and troop upstairs to bed.
It has been a pleasant evening
in a civilized city.

Most of the young people in the room
will die young;
but luckily
they imagine for themselves
a long life.

AT THE POET'S BIRTHPLACE

Will the ghost of the dead poet
be put off by all that scrubbing and polishing
the house has had since he lived in it?
Or by the crowds of the faithful
buying postcards and guidebooks?
A ghost, one imagines, likes things as they were.

Still, familiar objects have been gathered,
locks of hair, snuff boxes,
a knife and fork he used, wine glasses,
a family Bible, scraps of poems, love letters,
even an oatcake cooked by the poet's wife,
preserved under glass. These may bring him back.
After all, hasn't the race always saved
dishes and food for the dead?

And there are portraits, real and imaginary,
of the poet, his wife, children, mistresses.
He was more rugged, more like a farmer,
than the portraits showed, they say.
And his eyes glowed, the young boy remembered
who spoke to him only once.
There were never such eyes
in any other man's head.

Ghost, ghost, you are more alive still
than half the people in this room.

RETURN OF THE NATIVE

This is the true land of fairy tales,
this countryside of sullen beauty
heavy beneath dark trees. The brown smell of wood
lingers about it. Sawdust penetrates
every corner. You smell it, mixed with manure,
in the restaurant with its moosehead, or, like dim must,
in the little movie house.

The short street swims in dust and sunshine, slides
into a country road, and crosses the bridge
across the log-filled river where men walk,
balancing on the logs, and a single rowboat
holds a group of boys, their dark, round heads
bent close together. Sunshine, wind, and water
carry together the floating smell of boards.

Across the bridge is pasture; later, woods.
This is a land
not settled yet by its generations of settlers.
Wildness still lingers, and the unfriendly trees
suffer, but do not shelter, man, their neighbour.
No Eden this, with parks and friendly beasts,
though hopeful settlers, not far distant, called
their country Canaan, New Jerusalem,
or even Beulah. Yet beauty here is solemn,
with the freshness of some strange and morning world.

At the last house on the edge of the woods, two children
sit on their swings, reading aloud to each other
a fairy tale of children in a wood.
Their mother, hanging up her Monday wash,
stops for a minute and watches flying over
the shining crows flapping their heavy wings.

VIEW FROM WINDOW

My small, clean room has pink wallpaper.
The bed is high and white.
On a ledge above the window
are six books
and a model of a sailing ship.

In the backyard
one hen wanders through grass
among dandelions.
Another scratches in the brown earth
with one leg,
bending her head for worms.
A dog barks in the distance.

Beyond the green picket fence
there is a road,
but not many cars travel it.

IMMIGRANTS

There are swans on the pond
instead of the ducks which once swam there.
Brought to the town by airplane
they are not native, winter with difficulty,
are superior fragile birds.

I admire
their white graceful throats,
their easy motions,
but somehow liked the ducks better.

THE POET IN THE LAST DAYS

I grow too old for love—
have never cared for money—
and fame is youth's delusion,
who read Catullus
and wanted to save, like him,
some one thing—a sparrow, maybe—
from the cold touch of time

a small brown quivering bird
frightened
or a day, night, pair of hands
with veins running blue and prominent,
or a mole on the neck, moved in and out with breath.

I wanted to save breath
hold it caught in,
not released
until sometime centuries later
I might breathe it out
blow the hair of
someone sitting reading
not expecting a ghost.

But I thought then
there would always be books,
there would be
lamps or candlelight,
there would always be people
reading at night,
lonely, stirring up the fire,
inviting the spirits of the dead

to tell them about sparrows
or the veins in hands
or the feel of a ballpoint pen
grasped in dead fingers.

But how can there be poems
if there are no sparrows
and no people?
How can a ghost haunt
a world without houses?

EARTHQUAKE

Sometimes there are earthquakes in the mind.
It cracks and heaves
shakes off its top layers
and shows below
metals, fire, granite,
rivers flowing in a changed direction.

And there are buried cities
revealed again
streets and houses
completely furnished
the dead in agonized poses
petrified
or locked in love's embrace.

There is a child's doll with a broken head
there is a round striped ball
there is a broom made of branches
a picnic basket lying abandoned
under a tree

some faded flags and uniforms
discoloured
war posters.

95

SEASONAL

One friend has killed himself; another dies
gradually operation by operation.
I too am breakable.
My flesh and bones have been renewed seven times
and yet they feel past scars and sprains.

Underground the mind is dark soil.
Through its cracks and crannies
silence seeps like rain.
Some time, after all that drought and hail,
the mind will be prairie in a good year,
will ripple wheat and lupines.

But what of the flesh, I ask?
What of the dead man's wounds?
What of your cancer-ridden cells?

What field of grain and poppies
can take the place of any pair of hands,
of the web of skin
covering bone, joint, and tendon?
Whose eyes will have
precisely the same colour in the iris?

But why do I grieve,
dying while I grieve?
The pattern of my atoms too will break.
Beyond the Milky Way
how many galaxies explode in light?

ON THE DEATH BY BURNING OF
KIMBERLY HAMMER, MAY 1972

Only the grandmother weeps—
the mother smiles, tearless,
the father also,
though panic clouds his eyes,
an effort
not to see.

A neighbour remembers
the child Kimberly
out walking at Christmas
wrapped for winter,
cheeks pink, eyes bright as candles,
saying,
"I like to walk in the cold. I like the cold."

When fire blazed through the tent,
when there was no cold,
did your young eyes see
all past and future blazing at once?

Knowing you will miss
our gradual years
the slow burn
of time in your flesh,
we are not sure
if what we feel is pity
or is envy.

Later, at night,
I awake cold in bed,
pile on winter blankets,
make a tent
of skin and blankets.

I sleep again, and dream
of you, Kimberly,
no child of mine, no relative,
a May candle
burning
in the dark.

JUDGMENT

The world is falling down.
Rocks crack and lava flows.
Trees break off from their banks,
are whirled down streams of flame.

Oh, where can I escape?

The voices of the dead
cry in the wind:
"Eden is buried,
there can be no return."

The voices of the unborn
never to be born
weep their betrayal:
there is no new heaven;
there will be no more sea.

WAITING ROOM

My father stands in front of me
as we ride upstairs on an escalator.

Upstairs a small girl and an old woman
chant together, Time Time Time Time.

I sit down beside the child.
We are both waiting
for someone on the other side of the closed door.

Through an open window
we see green trees in an orchard.

Night is falling.
My father is somewhere else.

LOST

I dream I am honeymooning with my father
in a strange city.
Somebody says the word "incest"
and I run away.

I cannot find my way
in all these labyrinths.
There are miles of empty shop windows.
My feet are bleeding.
I carry my shoes in my hands.

I am not sure
if I am escaping from my father
or trying to find him again.

WILDERNESS DREAM

The girl and the man in the dream
wear animal skins, are hunters,
camp all night in a shack
in the wilderness.

It is a northern landscape
rugged.
The trees grow low
but hardy.

Ghosts come, ghosts of Indian warriors,
and encircle the camp.
There are strange wizard spirits
hobgoblins
dangerous
with candle eyes.

Nevertheless,
the man and the girl will survive,
are protected from ghosts

because—

There is some magic reason
but the dream did not reveal it.

DISQUALIFICATION

I am of puritan and loyalist ancestry
and of middle-class tastes.
My father never swore in front of ladies,
as he always quaintly called women.
My mother thought that a man was no gentleman
if he smoked a cigar without asking her permission;
and she thought all men should be gentlemen,
even though a gentleman would not call himself one,
and all women should be ladies,
even though a lady would not call herself one.

I have never taken any drug
stronger than aspirin.
I have never been more than slightly drunk.
I think there are worse vices
than hypocrisy or gentility
or even than voting Conservative.

If I wanted to be fucked
I should probably choose a different word.
(Anyhow, I am not quite sure
whether it is a transitive or an intransitive verb,
because it was never given to me to parse.)

Usually I can parse words, analyse sentences,
spell, punctuate,
and recognize the more common metrical forms.

It is almost impossible
that I shall ever be
a truly established poet.

PILGRIM

I shall visit the Holy Land
(the child said)
I shall carry a blue pitcher
on my head

I shall be Rebekah
at the well
I shall wear gold bracelets
and they will jangle

I shall be the Shulamite
I shall be Egypt's daughter
I shall marry Solomon
and die and live thereafter

I shall be the lady
who lived with seven men
she who gave water to the stranger
and was comforted again

I shall live in the old time
before I was born
and I shall turn again
turn and return

SOMETIMES I THINK OF MOVING

I: The Silent Scream

FOR PAT LOWTHER

Hearing of your death
in violence
your body found by a fisherman
drifting
as in your floating
Protean poem,
I realize you must have dreamed
just this death

and in my own dreams lately
you have walked white-faced,
blood on your forehead,
wearing a seaweed-black
trailing skirt

but speaking
in a voice
gentle as water
your tidal poems.

And I remember
that this summer I envied you
your poems,
their gull-and-falcon swooping,
and even the pain behind them
that poured blood into them.

Forgive me, gentle ghost.
Haunt my mind's
passageways
with your grace.
Haunt me with your words.
Let your spilled blood
renew my veins.

Rise, and walk
on all the waters
of your tears,
like sunshine stepping
on the waves
of the life-and-death-creating
end-of-all-journeys sea.

THE PHOTOGRAPHER

The photographer has placed
all the proofs for my photographs
on one sheet
so that there are twelve versions
of one person
smiling   sad   serious
sideways
dead on
all looking at me at once.

How can I choose from all these faces?
Is one more authentic than the others?
I remember he said (after that one)
"This isn't a bloody funeral, is it?
Am I a dentist?"
(The reason for the teeth in the next one)

"The trouble is," he said,
"a photograph is flat
and you have another dimension.
Right?"

So there is a problem of placement.
And there is also the problem
of making the pose seem casual
so that he needs to come and tilt the chin
at just the correct angle
for casualness

(That I understand)

So here are the results
these twelve faces
all of which are in a way authentic
and in a way fake

But the ones that look most natural
(and maybe are)
are the ones the photographer
worked hardest to pose.

BIOGRAPHY AND THE POET
A poem for Cathy

Why, someone asks,
this intrusion
of the poet's life?
Why isn't the poem
separate and anonymous
as the bridge across a river
which exists only to support
its burden of cars and people?
Who cares about the poet
any more than about the engineer?

Maybe because
poems after all
are not made of steel or concrete,
are not shaped with the aid of blueprints,
cannot be duplicated
over another river.

Poems are more organic:
at worst excremental,
at best like children,
separate but wearing
the parental features;
sometimes maybe plants,
green mysteries
springing unexpected
from the heart's humus.

It's a more real presence, maybe,
this red maple,
than the bones of the dead poet
feeding its roots;

but be careful how you crush
under your fingers
these brittle wafer leaves
which look dry and powdery.

You might break through to flesh.
Your whole hand might be
sopped in blood.

TO THE MALE MUSE

What other friend or lover,
after all, would have been so faithful (more or less)
as you have been all these years?
Putting up with TV dinners
and ice cream because it's easy.
Putting up with my long monologue
about myself,
the endlessly accumulating details,
the turn and return
on the same themes.
Putting up with my restlessness,
my moves here and moves there,
always to boring places
Sackville instead of Bangkok
Saskatoon instead of Athens.

Oh, I'll admit
I've been jealous of you at times.
You take the other girls to fancier restaurants
show off more for them
use a smoother line
(I suppose you know
I like something simple:
there's no point trying new tricks
when I like the old ones just as well)

Sometimes you've deserted me
as sometimes I've deserted you.
I can't complain.
Neither of us is the marrying type.

But you come back.
You know you're comfortable with me
and that I drop everything and everybody else
whenever you ring me up.

True love
is always requited.

In spite of anything I may have said
all my love letters
have been written
to you.

THE SILENT SCREAM

When I was seven, playing by myself
near the edge of the woods,
I was almost buried in a pile of sawdust
that gave way spungily into quicksand.
As I sank up to my neck, struggling,
I opened my mouth to scream.
But my voice had gone.

I got out. I survived. Did not tell my mother
or anyone else for over twenty years.
Dreamed, however,
many times of being buried alive,
nose and mouth choked with earth or sawdust,
no voice ever
because I could not scream.

I wonder if that is why all the reviewers
say I am such a quiet poet.

ERMINE

My brother caught a weasel
in one of his rabbit snares,
gave me the skin, saying,
"Now you have ermine,
the same as the queen wears,
or the rich movie stars."

And I would not believe him at first
until my parents said,
"Yes, yes, it's true,
he's not teasing you.
Ermine is weasel skin."

Then I stroked the white fur,
dressed my dolls with it,
so that each became in turn
Mary Queen of Scots
or my namesake Elizabeth
stepping on Raleigh's cloak

or maybe some other
more barbaric queen
who felt, when she wore it,
the stiff pink inside of the skin
and rejoiced to own
the weasel's sharp presence
its small fierce head.

MAGNOLIA AVENUE

The name of the street was Magnolia Avenue,
but there were never any magnolias on it.
In the spring it was muddy.
Snot-nosed Dotty lived next door.
Wearing rubber boots, she waded
in the wet brown ooze, called out to me,
"Come on in, the water's fine."
There was beautiful thick mud that morning
all over my stockings.
My mother scolded, called me away inside.

I climbed the stairway from the front hallway
to slide down the banister all afternoon,
once, twice, a dozen, twenty times.
"You'll hurt yourself," my mother called, grumbling.
"You'll ruin your flowered panties."

I fell asleep playing with paper dolls.

In the evening after supper
I stood by the kitchen window eating cake
looking across at the window of Dotty's house.
Dotty's mother had black lace curtains.
They were drawn tight. Nobody looked out.

"Come away from the window," Mother said.
"Someone will think you're spying."

I never saw the inside of that room
and it was years before I saw magnolias.

CHILD PLAYING WITH BALL

The little girl
pats the ball
up and down
up and down
trying to go on patting
as long as she can,
counting the pats.

The mother does not like it
this monotony of sound
but the little girl likes it,
up-and-down up-and-down
a rhythm
like skipping
or swinging
or the heart beating
when you run

or the sweep and rush
of the soft, monotonous,
down-slanting, pattering
patting
rain.

REASONS FOR REASON

My father used to tell me
that one of his first memories
was of walking past the old Saint John Asylum
beneath the window of a girl
who shook the bars
and screamed,
"I'll kill you, boy!
Boy, I'll kill you!"

and my mother sometimes showed me the scar
that Cousin Bethiah made
when she went crazy
and chased my mother around the kitchen table
with a butcher knife
before the uncles caught her
and she was taken away

and when I was a child
I read in the Saint John paper
the investigations of that asylum
the lock-and-bolt treatments
the filth, the blows, the straitjackets

so of course I try
to be as reasonable myself as possible,
make sure the butcher knife
is not too sharp
and put it away
as soon as I can
after carving.

IN FAVOUR OF BEING ALIVE

Twenty-four years ago
I tried to kill myself
but with my usual incompetence
did not manage to.

Not even one good poem
out of it.
Obviously
I was no Sylvia Plath.

I don't know
why I write about it now
(and even now
I am not giving details)

except maybe I write
for hortatory or didactic reasons
to say to someone
Don't!

It's been a dull life
much of the time
but lots better
than no life at all.

You don't know how much
you may yet enjoy
just waking up
and peeling oranges
to eat with sugar
while you listen to the clock strike
down at the Town Hall
telling you again
that you're still here

and Sylvia Plath isn't.

AFTERMATH OF THE *TITANIC*

If I were to write a poem about the *Titanic*
(as, after Pratt, I don't think I shall)
I think I would choose that moment
just after the ship had gone down
when the great cry rose up from the water
of the drowning freezing
knowing now their false
useless courage
now that the ship was broken
and the band no longer played

and the half-empty lifeboats
pushed away
from the cries of the drowning,
the screams they would never forget
which would come back in nightmares
all their lives.

Or maybe I would write
about that lifeboat full of women
that pulled a drunken stoker on board
and could only keep him quiet
by taking turns sitting on him
(I like to think of those fat
stodgy practical women
no pretence of heroism
but weighed down
by heavy titanic dinners)

Or the investigations later
recriminations, rumours true and false.
Did the captain kill himself?
Was the ship speeding
because one of the company directors
wanted to make New York
in time for a dinner date?
Did the *Californian*
see those signals
and ignore them?

I might speak
of the great usefulness
of the wreck for the newspapers
back in those peaceful doldrum days
two years before the War.

And yes I would write
how for months thereafter
ships were wary
of that stretch
of the Atlantic,
sailors thought it haunted
by lights and voices

and passengers were disturbed
when ships encountered
(as they did sometimes)
the bodies of the dead
unrecognizable
floating
upheld by life preservers.

MIRAGE

Always it is elsewhere
never here
or if ever here
never to be held.

In my dreams
there are airports, palm trees
a hot pink city somewhere
by green waves

a mirage

The widow tells me
about that summer with her husband
in a sunny cottage by the Mediterranean
where she learned to do wonders
cooking at the fireplace
simmering the chicken in wine
because wine was so cheap;

the hot days, the cool nights,
dinner by the fire,
the fisherman's children
serenading them in the evening
for a few coins
or in the daytime clustering
around her husband's typewriter
like little flies
while he typed and sweated.

All this she remembers fondly,
I see she can almost touch
those evenings
the leaping shadows
of firelight on the walls
or the daytime walks
through the hot white sand.

And we sit together
each remembering
separately
our separate constructs.

It is a painting I remember
of pink crumbling houses.

I was never there.

FROM MY DREAM NOTEBOOK

Have been dreaming frequently
about moving
into an unfinished cottage.
No panes in the windows.
Fresh air blows in.
I pick books up
off the floor,
pile them on shelves

or I go walking
by the ocean/river/lake.

There is a village
rather small
with wooden shops.
A crossroads.
A railway track.
A hill.
Farming country.

I get lost
and have to ask my way.
People answer in French.

It is somewhere
somewhere East
in maybe the Laurentians
or maybe by the Atlantic.

I have come
after all
to live with my lover
though I do not see him
and am not sure who he is.

I think
I have only ten more years to live
but I am resigned,
accept my death—

that is, in my dream I do.

ON THE VALUE OF FANTASIES

The teacher on the morning radio program
disapproves because her girl students
have such unrealistic fantasies.
They all think they will go to college,
marry a lawyer or a professor,
have two kids and two cars,
and live happily ever after.

And she gets them to play a game
in which Linda becomes a widow at fifty,
Paulette is deserted at thirty-five
and has to bring up four kids
on a steno's salary, and poor Jennifer
never marries at all.
How will they cope?

Of course it's a matter of
one fantasy against another;
and sometimes it's fun
to imagine oneself bearing up against adversity.

Myself, though, I agree with the kids
that it's rather a dumb game.
It's true, life is full of these dirty tricks,
but being prepared for the worst may make it happen.

(More might be said
for fantasizing about space travel
or maybe about being a mermaid.)

I still hope (two months before my fifty-third birthday)
that I may yet meet that handsome stranger
all the fortune tellers have told me about;
that sometime my lottery ticket
will win a tax-free fortune,
and that my poems become household words
and make the next edition of Colombo's *Quotations.*

I might as well believe in heaven, too,
for all the good it will do me to admit
statistics are against it.

LADY WITH A CREATIVE IMAGINATION

Sometimes in her stories her father was lavishly wealthy,
drove six limousines, lived in a ninety-room house
designed by a famous architect, with Picassos on the walls,
and all the books first editions signed by their authors,
as, "Lovingly, Hemingway" or "Cheers, Somerset
    Maugham."
She was weaned on champagne, cut her first tooth on
    diamond,
and was baptized in a christening robe
purchased from an exiled Romanoff princess
who had carried it with her
as she escaped from Russia
in the disguise of a washerwoman.

But other times she said her father was a fisherman,
very poor, from the coast of Newfoundland.
She was brought up on potatoes, fish, and folk songs,
and never saw an electric light until she was nineteen.

Sometimes she pictured herself as a brilliant scholar,
publishing articles in unspecified periodicals,
graduate of only the best-known universities,
with at least two doctorates in different fields.
At other times she scorned the academic world,
had stopped school at the eighth grade,
learned all she knew from life and not from books,
but anyhow was writing two novels and a play.

                    And some people said she was
B.A. with second-class honours
from the University of Manitoba,
her father owner of a small-town hardware store,
no luxury or hardship in her life.

Still, she created one fine work of fiction—
that was herself.

MAN WHO WAS HALF BEAR

The bear-man born near my home town
back in the nineteenth century—
what was he like?
The correspondent to the local paper
says he was gentle, tractable,
but liked to sleep on shavings,
caught fish with his bare hands.
When he was grown up
he joined a circus
and travelled to the States,
faded from the ken of his kin.

Now, there are all those unanswered questions
about identity.
What about his mother?
Is this just one of those birthmark stories
where the pregnant wife
runs from the blueberry patch
and can't forget the bear?
Or was she raped—
seduced possibly—
by a jovial brown beast
with more hair on his chest
than most lovers?
What did she think
of her mild, uncouth son
when his ponderous baby footsteps
shook the house?
or his large paw swiped against her china cupboards?

I see him going courting,
his curly mane slicked down
with bear's grease,
bending to growl a compliment
into some small pink ear

hopelessly hopelessly
for girls would never love him.

I see his eyes perplexed.

Did he try the woods then,
think he might live
in ferny hollows or dark caves?
But he did not know bear language,
had acquired a taste
for cooked food,
porridge with his honey.

That other bear-boy, Beowulf,
could kill monsters with his naked hands,
win rings and armour,
but our boy lived
at the wrong time in the wrong place
for epic virtues.

Oh, he was lost,
not belonging
here or there,
was neither tame nor wild,
fit only
to be a circus freak

poor boy, poor man,
poor gentle bear

125

II: Where I Come From

KITE DREAM

Circling deep in the woods under the boughs of night,
bare feet sinking in moss, slipping in moist pathways,
branches scratching my arms and bruising my lips, I move
down to the water's edge.

Sudden bright in the sun whitecaps on blue dazzle.
All is open and wide, free as the wind, with tossed
wheatfields of water rippling under the hot
eye of the morning

and I now am a child, flying a paper kite
over waters of time, prairies of mind, far back
to the self before me or forward to life, the future,
wind blowing onward now

126

WHERE I COME FROM

People are made of places. They carry with them
hints of jungles or mountains, a tropic grace
or the cool eyes of sea-gazers. Atmosphere of cities
how different drops from them, like the smell of smog
or the almost-not-smell of tulips in the spring,
nature tidily plotted in little squares
with a fountain in the centre; museum smell,
art also tidily plotted with a guidebook;
or the smell of work, glue factories maybe,
chromium-plated offices; smell of subways
crowded at rush hours.

             Where I come from, people
carry woods in their minds, acres of pine woods;
blueberry patches in the burned-out bush;
wooden farmhouses, old, in need of paint,
with yards where hens and chickens circle about,
clucking aimlessly; battered schoolhouses
behind which violets grow. Spring and winter
are the mind's chief seasons: ice and the breaking of ice.

A door in the mind blows open, and there blows
a frosty wind from fields of snow.

WOMAN ON A BUS:
IN NEW BRUNSWICK WOODS

No, I'm not used to it yet, though it's over forty years.
My husband was a soldier in the War,
came from these parts. You know how it was in the War.
We were sorry for the boys so far from home,
and England was dreary then, with all the rationing,
and the cold, and the shortages. This country sounded good,
and Ed looked good in uniform. He said I'd never be sorry.

Look at all those woods. Ed thought it pretty country,
but I never got used to all that fir and spruce
and the trees going on for miles and miles.
Not the kind of woods you walk in, like at home.

I used to walk in the woods when I first came over,
go out and sing to myself there, but they thought I was crazy,
and so I stopped. My, how I used to cry
back in those early days. Some women went back;
but there—I'd married Ed, and I'd stick by him.

Well, he was a good man in his way,
never got drunk to speak of, never swore
when I was around. He couldn't help the country
being the way it is.

            What I really wanted
was something, now, like Brighton.
I had a holiday there when I was young—
stayed nearly a week—that was a jolly time.
Brighton was grand. That's when I was in service
not far from there. But there's nothing like that here.

Look at the dark, how it's come on so sudden.
They have no twilight here, as they have at home.
She dips and is gone. There are no softnesses,
but only black and brightness.

No, even the violets here don't have the smell
they did at home, when you walked down the road
in the April night and smelled them.

Now that Ed's gone, I think sometimes of going
back home and seeing it. But I'm afraid
maybe the country isn't what it was.
I wouldn't know my sisters. All my children
live in these parts. And maybe—
I don't know—
when I got over there I'd miss the woods.

EQUALS

The least popular Canadian Prime Minister
my father's second cousin
(so my father called him, I don't know
the family tree)
went to school with him
in the Hopewell Cape School,
Dick Bennett one of the big boys,
my father seven years younger.

I saw old R.B.
in Sussex, New Brunswick
in the late thirties, on his last trip
across the country before he left it for good

and I remember
the two men standing together,
my father stooped with failure
in his shabby suit
trying to maintain
some dignity with the great man
(after all, he could still call him Dick)

and the portly, erect, balding
rich man
ex-Calgary lawyer
ex-Prime Minister
warily polite
to a poor relation
in case he might be asked for a loan
not needing votes any longer
but wishing to be agreeable

to say yes yes he remembered
those were great days
when we were boys
and this is your little girl

and I compared the two men painfully
thinking the only likeness
was the blue
sea-gazing eyes
of their Fundy boyhood

but now I realize
they were more alike than I thought
both mothers' boys
yearning for a home they could not return to

both failed men, bitter,
overcome by circumstance,
remembering their enemies
turning over their failure
in their minds

but the bigger failure
that of the man
who had travelled farther.

Maybe more to be pitied, that old man
stubbornly moving to a home not really home,
his last years filled with unimportant work
time-filling
or spent going from one movie to another
in wartime London
his best-loved kinsfolk dead.

Both of those men dead now for years.
Asleep.
Dreaming, maybe
of the shore at the Cape
still the way they remembered it,
projecting rocks
shaped by the stroke of waves,
blue-and-cream water,
the marvellous caves, hidden
from easy sight

the Bay deep enough
to drown any failure.

WHALES

When whales are tired of the sea
sometimes they swim ashore,
climb up on the land to die;
they are just bored with water,
can't stand it any more,
must breathe in a different element
even if they die for it.

People, too,
cluster by water,
sit gazing out at it for hours,
dream about it when it is miles away.
They would like some time
to walk off a cliff and breathe
water or empty space
a different element.

SCENES FROM AN ABANDONED NOVEL

I

A large, airy room
catching the afternoon sun;
bow windows
overlooking the branches of trees.
In one corner an old desk
with pigeon-holes;
shelves above the pigeon-holes
holding a few books,
postcards,
a crystal candlestick
with a yellow candle
partly burned down.

Walls done in blue;
brown carpet, slightly worn;
sofa and stuffed chair, neutral.
Pictures on the wall, muted.

I can see the room.
It is waiting.
But I do not know
who lives there.
A woman, two women maybe?
I cannot see clearly.

2

This is the view from the window
of that room.

The woman looks downhill
at a collection of wooden houses
in the small town;

large, comfortable houses
with gables and bow windows,
long verandahs
where people sit on summer Sunday afternoons.

Behind the house a marshy field
which at this season (late April)
still has patches of snow.

The woman is waiting
for something or someone.
Will he come?

If I want to
I can make him.

3

She goes for a walk, alone,
still wearing her winter coat.
The streets and sidewalks
are bare of snow, but muddy.
The snow is shrinking
in the fields outside the village.

Some boys are playing
with a homemade kite
constructed of brown wrapping-paper.

What is in her mind?
What does she think of
when she sees
a kite flying in spring?

4

Introducing a character:
the typical English professor—
call him Andrew?
Elaborately casual in a tweed jacket
with leather elbows.
Smokes a pipe
occasionally
takes snuff in an eighteenth-century manner.
Is on guard
that his speech should not always be grammatical.
Elegant, but not on his dignity.
Manner mild.

Is the woman in love with him?
No, I think merely likes him,
perhaps confides in him about
whatever she has to confide.

5

A large room
dark in the daytime because
shaded by trees,
but cheerful at night
with the shades drawn
and a fire in the fireplace.

Polished floors,
bright rugs,
large heavy furniture.

A preference for
strong primary colours,
orange, red, green.

Bookcases of metal;
books, chiefly modern.
Painting, abstract.

Who lives here?
Is he the woman's lover?
Future, past, present?

I have not decided.

6

Another character:
a foil for Andrew
(call him Roger).
Green velvet jacket, dirty linen,
unkempt hair.
Drives a rattly Volkswagen.
Complains of the fleas
in his filthy flat.
Boasts of the girls he slept with
in Greece on his holiday,
but has none here.
(Are those others invented?)

Everybody laughs at Roger.

If I want to surprise my reader,
I should have him become
gradually
my hero.

But I think not.
I think he is just a foil.

137

7

The haunted house:
heavy, ancient furniture;
crimson chesterfield;
window filled with ferns,
their leaves spidery;
piano at one end of room
covered with photographs
of the dead;
Victorian books
in the small bookcase.

Why has the woman come to visit
this old house?
Does the novel threaten
to become Gothic?

8

There could be a scene
in which she weeps and he swears
(or perhaps he weeps and she swears?)

They should be at cross-purposes.

They converge upon each other
each to the other's destruction
like ship and iceberg.

What colour are her eyes?

Why do they never
make any jokes?

9

The college is
small liberal arts
and full of characters.
The village is small
and full of weather
and not much else.

It is a Chekhov town
in the provinces
yearning for Moscow
or Toronto.

Last week
somebody's wife
eloped with somebody else's husband
not because they loved one another
or even because they were much attracted
but because they were bored.

At least it was more amusing
than marking freshman essays.

No wonder my protagonist
suffers from ennui.
No wonder I cannot
take this novel anywhere.

OTTAWA SUMMERS

Back in the fifties I lived in Ottawa
and I walked by the Canal and I was lonely
as the ghost of poor Archie Lampman,
and I too wept for my lost love,
and got religion, and felt guilty and unabsolved.

And it is all long ago and was a great waste of time
even at that time.

Nothing much is left now
of either the love or the guilt or the religion;
but I remember the Canal, the brown water,
and the body of a dead dog that I once saw floating in it,
and I remember a ragged man
asleep on a park bench.

On the other side of the Canal,
in front of a monastery,
the young black-cassocked men
paced up and down, reading, I suppose,
their breviaries.

And we were all, God knows, lonely
as the ghost of poor Archie Lampman
walking this same town
dreaming of his Kate.

ROAD BETWEEN SASKATOON AND EDMONTON

Yes—there are hills on the prairie,
trees, even; the road sometimes winds.
It is not
home on the range
with perpetually sunny skies,
for up there in that sky
wider and higher than the one I grew up with
clouds shift and reshift,
drop sudden showers,
vanish again in sunlight.

I name over the foreign words and objects:
those almost-lakes are sloughs;
that is a windbreak of poplars,
geometrically planted before the square farmhouse.
The chief difference in the land
is that there is more of it.

The little towns are prairie clichés,
each with its grain elevator
onion-domed church
and Chinese restaurant.

But there are hints of Celtic landscape
near Kitscoty and Innisfree
lake water set in valleys
Irish and wet,
with new green grass,
and I can even imagine
the nine bean-rows
and a homesick immigrant
almost finding himself at home.

Will I ever be at home in this country?
Will I ever be at home again away from it?

WESTWARD THROUGH ALBERTA

Westward through Alberta
green and tawny
grain land, oil land
under the blue, white-dappled sky

miles of bush land
green trees silvering
when wind moves their leaves
in the summer sunlight

fields of yellow flowers,
green rounded hills,
cattle by water,
horses flicking tails.

Ten-minute stop
to walk up and down
the station platform
and stare at the grain elevator.

Then more bush
more water
grain cocks shaped
like loaves of bread

brown fields,
tractors,
a brown dirt road
going up hill.

Real woods now,
hills, valleys, chasms,
a waterfall,
purple fireweed
on the slopes.

We are out of the plains,
will wake in the mountains.
The sun has set
in the land of sunset

new world tomorrow.

RESURRECTION IN VANCOUVER

Sitting in Stanley Park
under a giant cedar
taller than any tree in Saskatoon,
looking out on all this Emily Carr greenness
and up to the gentle blue
of the sky beyond,
I am bathed in moist sunshine,
a soothing light,
and half wonder
if I might have died after all
on the train from the prairies
and been raised up again
in a Pacific Eden.

Surely that fat little boy
with a green balloon
is a remarkably solid cherub;
the young men with beards
are risen prophets,
and angels wander here and there
in long skirts or in slacks.

But I think
(watching the fountain playing)
if I had really died,
I should have enough friends here
so that at least one would materialize
lying sprawled under that willow tree
or come strolling down the path
to tell me the way to the rose garden
or where I could find the peacocks.

I can think of one or two spirits
who would probably suggest
a beer in the pavilion.

I remember my sister told me
of dreaming she had died
and was cruising through bland seas
toward an exclusive resort;
everything handsome and luxurious about her,
a lavish stateroom, decidedly first-class,
and people dancing on deck to exclusive music.

But the other passengers
all looked through her
as though she were not there;
she did not recognize a single soul;
and she sat in a deck chair weeping
all the way
into the harbour.

144

SLEEPING BY SECHELT INLET

Sleeping by Sechelt Inlet
in a house overlooking the water
half-waking to the sound of water
slapping
on the carved rocks
and the bobbing wooden float

sleeping in a house full of children dreaming
turning and sighing in their sleep

with the cool balsam-smelling darkness flowing
around the sleepers
through the open door

and sounds of rustlings
in the woods behind the house:

half-sleeping, dreaming
I dreamed a dream of touching
reaching hands

and in my dream I said,
"This is no dream, because
in dreams I could not touch;
and see, I do,
I touch
your hands.
I am not dreaming.
This is real."

ON MY WAY HOME

Waking on the train,
sitting up in my berth,
I raise the blind,
suddenly see the wide, swaying
plain, the wide grey sky

and I am glad
at last
to be out of the beautiful
claustrophobic mountains

(though I admired,
I apologize to the mountains
if I seem to criticize them)

Now I am glad
to see the landscape running
open and free and without barriers

and I wash my face and dress
in the shiplike rolling train
and pack for the station

and I am glad
I am on my way
home

146

III: Map of the City

SUMMERS HERE AND THERE

June is cold this year.
Rain and wind bend the green billowing trees.
A lawn chair left on the balcony
would likely blow away.

And I am homesick for somewhere
where it's really summer,
for blowsy heatwave days
with drooping peonies on humid lawns

and willows trailing
their green sweating hair
in river water

or even for streets
where men with carts
sell ice-cream cones
at corners
and someone plunks a tune
on a guitar
and artists draw
for a few coins
with chalk on sidewalk.

I remember somewhere
some time
hot fragrant nights
the hot chirr
of a crickety insect sound
and the damp smell of earth
steaming up to my window.

And now that time is here for me.
I have created it
out of the smell of rain
and the slithering sound
of the cars sliding past
on the wet street

dark coming on
this cold June
I come back to.

148

NEW GLASSES

New glasses. Everything bright again. I can see
signs at street corners and the names of buses
and am pleased at the richness
of the red brick of the church hall
and the white of that patch of daisies
in a rock garden
I never noticed before.

I think
I will go all over town
and look at the paint on houses
and notice the pattern
of the old-man dandelion heads.

And I am surprised how pretty
the waitress in the teashop is,
how becoming her green uniform,
and I think I must look again
at the faces of all my acquaintance
and the wrinkles of old women at street corners.

just at the moment I pity
people with perfect vision
who have never worried about going blind
and who never experience
this joy of fresh sight
and the marvel
of the old world made new again
and yet again

how many times
since I wore my first pair of glasses
when I was fourteen.

MAP OF THE CITY

"Beautiful Saskatoon,
potash capital of the world,"

the map is labelled.

No population figures given
but 135,000 in January 1975
so they say at the Public Library.

On the front of the map, in colour,
Saskatoon on a late June day.
View across the bridge from the south side of the river
to the Bessborough Hotel,
a fortress Gothic
as the early twentieth century
could build,
guarding the city hall
some shops and churches;
beyond, green fields,
and above, the sky as blue and infinite
as when I look out at it now
from my window
(after that thunderstorm in the night).

See, when you open the map
it is divided
almost exactly in two
by the slant of
the South Saskatchewan River
running from corner to corner.

From my side (north)
and the shops, police station, post office
I cross daily
over one of these bridges.
The map does not show
the cars, trucks, bicycles, buses
and how they creep at rush hour
and it does not show the bridge on a windy day
or the fine dust blowing
into the mouths of pedestrians.

On the north side
the streets are mostly numbered
(except for Saskatchewan Crescent
by the river
and some on the far outskirts)
but on the south side
there are also streets with names:
University Drive and College,
and Temperance to remind us
that Saskatoon was founded
by Methodist Total Abstainers
from Ontario;

Colony and Garrison
(how Canadian);

and to the far south
a group of streets named for girls and trees:
Isabella, Adelaide, Ruth,
Maple, Willow, Elm, Ash.

Almost off the map,
on the right,
are streets named
Harvard, Cambridge, Yale,
McGill, Carleton,
Dalhousie, Mount Allison,
Waterloo, McMaster,
Simon Fraser.

The map shows
parks, open spaces, transit systems, schools,
It lists
recreation units, swimming pools,
rinks,
cemeteries:

does not show, however,
houses, gardens, trees,
the *Star-Phoenix* office,
the naval barracks,
old women out with shopping baskets,
children on a merry-go-round
or riding the toy train
in Kinsmen's Park.

152

SOMETIMES I THINK OF MOVING

Sometimes I think of moving
to the other side of the river,
where the lawns are sleeker
and I could walk
to the university.

But then I take my Saturday walk
past the Co-op
and the Mennonite Clothing Store
and the Army and Navy

and within sight of
the Early Seeds and Feeds
grain elevator
I am stranded on a traffic island
in the midst of the street
while a big truck passes
full of pigs
smelling as pigs do
and then a wedding party
in a car crowned with flowers
the driver leaning wildly
on his horn

and I am released
and walk along Twentieth Street
past Ukrainian and Greek restaurants
and pawnshops and furniture shops
and Ben's Bad Books.

I peer into a shop
smelling of spicy meats
and crusty homemade bread
in unwrapped loaves

and in Paul's Music Store
I poke among Ukrainian souvenirs
made in Germany
and Canadian souvenirs
made in Japan
and T-shirts bearing the plea
"Kiss me. I'm Ukrainian"
(made in Montreal?)

and I buy a record
of Canada's National Ukrainian Choir
of Dauphin
because after all this is a bilingual country

isn't it?

I walk as far as
one of the two Ukrainian churches
when I meet another wedding party
with more cars and more horns

and I plunge down a side street
past backyard gardens
with petunias and bleeding hearts
and marigolds and pansies.

An old Chinese woman
is cutting flowers

154

and the wind is wildly blowing
the branches of trees

the sun is burning.

There is dust in my mouth
and in my eyes
and my feet are beginning to hurt
and I am happy

and I walk home past City Hall
thinking I will not move yet
from my side of the river.

155

I LIKE TO VISIT THE MENDEL ART GALLERY

I like to visit the Mendel Art Gallery
not so much on account of the art
(though there are the usual Eskimo carvings
and Group of Seven paintings
and I admire
that Lawren Harris landscape
that looks like ice cream
in a cone of pure ice)

but in summer I like the walk
to the Gallery through the park
past a ball-game in progress
and picnic tables
and people lying flat
face down in the grass
with the sun pouring down on them

and in the Gallery the tourists
and the summer children
and the view out the window
onto the river
and onto a green lane
with a cyclist riding down it.

And summer or winter
I like to step down
into the little
glassed-in conservatory
full of tropical plants

156

steamy in winter
cool in summer
humming with fans
surrounding you with
the green smell
of chlorophyll.

Oh, it is a marvell-
ous shady place

of umbrella trees
birdsnest ferns
birdcatcher trees
Norfolk pines

and flowers of Arrow Root
from Brazil,
some purple, some white,
like huge violets
and a cactus with a yellow bloom
called Irish-mittens
from Argentina

jade-plants from Natal

and in the centre
a banana tree
with clusters of green bananas
that mothers point out to their children

and all the while the fountain plays
into the moist tropical air

and, winter or summer,
in spite of gales and snow
and dust storms and hail
it is paradisal summer
here.

OUTDOOR MARKET, SASKATOON

The outdoor market behind the City Hall
is not much as outdoor markets go

just a few stalls
for people selling eggs
and homemade cookies and yoghurt,
a table with pottery,
some embroidered aprons

and I miss those big markets
with handsome cheeses
and amber slabs of maple sugar
and fresh fish for sale
and new-picked fiddleheads
and bunches of Sweet William
and a box full of somebody's kittens.

But a market of any size
should be encouraged;
so at least I will buy a dozen eggs
from this girl in her flowered dress
with fair flying hair

and hope for her sake
that the crazy wind
will not topple all the stalls
blow away the aprons
and send the eggs crashing
to the ground.

158

DOMINION DAY, SASKATOON

The most perfect day of summer.
Families with children
lining the river bank

and near the old Hotel
a platform with someone making a speech
about This Canada of Ours

and a pipe band of youngsters in kilts
marching up and down
playing highland tunes
in front of a booth selling
corn on the cob and cabbage rolls and
varenyky with cream.

A Ford Model-T drives up
with the sheriff of Boomtown
and ladies from the Western Development Museum
wearing Victorian dresses

and everybody gives them a big hand.

Somebody is doing a good business
selling old lamps and teapots
and cracked vases
cleared out of attics.

Meanwhile, it's cooler
if you turn the corner
down to Kiwanis Park
where crowds of people sit on grass
or on the benches
in the shade
while a band takes a long time
to tune up.

Finally it begins to play
O Canada
and we gradually stand up
in a ragged
self-conscious line

everybody except
this one Indian boy
face down, fast asleep
with his shoes off
lying at my feet
in the waving grass.

160

ORDINARY EVIL

Even Saskatoon is not as cosy
as I sometimes like to think it.
Four children murdered here this summer
by a twenty-seven-year-old truckdriver,
somebody ordinary and nondescript,
nobody special.

Sexual assault,
or did he just revenge himself
for something done to him
when he was a child?

"He must have been crazy,"
we all say,
avoiding each other's eyes,
wondering
about ourselves and each other.

Would anybody want
to murder me?
Is there nobody I have wished
(oh, only for a moment)
out of my way?

FRIDAY NIGHT

I sit eating potato chips
covered with grease
from the carton.
They need salt.

What shall I do
with the evening?
What shall I do with my life?

On page one of tonight's paper
is a picture of children fishing
in the Saskatchewan River.
Their lines dangle.
The fish are not biting.

SUNDAY MORNING

I feel
sloppy and shapeless as an old housecoat
and I get up late
and pad about the apartment
in greying terry slippers.
I have not bothered to shave my legs.

Joylessly, I do bending exercises
attempt

Mind
can no longer do handsprings
    (and never could either
        I tell myself)

Is it too late
after all
for the necessary conversion
which was to have changed my life?
Could I still not become
beautiful
as a lady on television
with come-hither eyelashes
(First lose ten pounds)
or become so liberated
that beauty is unnecessary?

Could I not still find
some formula
(meter breath projective
villanelles)
to provide the perfect poem
foolproof   reviewer-proof

and make sure my next novel
is not autobiographical?

Or could I take up watercolours
and not have to worry about words

Or some people say
wonderful results can be obtained
by simply being unselfish.

Life is not worse
than when I was twenty
I remind myself.
It's just that I am an incurable dreamer
and would like it to be perfect.

Clouds billow away
from a patch of pale June sky.
Even the smallest insect
resting on a sunny wall
with no purpose in life
and no standing in the community
knows enough to be happy.

REFLECTIONS

Living by myself, listening
to the hum of my refrigerator
or the tinned radio voice,
or looking out my window
at birds on the church roof,
hearing the birds in the distance,
or hearing the screech of a car's brakes
which startles and disperses them

I remember the argument
that what is not seen or heard
does not exist.

How many pairs of eyes
see the birds,
which are now invisible to me?
At the moment, nobody sees me.
I see my own hand
holding my pen
writing on the lined page.
Therefore my hand exists.

On Monday I can go to the office,
write memos, talk to students.
There is always the telephone.

There are three mirrors
in my apartment.
If I broke them all,
would I still be here?

IV: The Dancers

THE DANCERS

I see in dreams the dancers
(Dance over, my lady Lee)
Dancing the games of childhood
Under the high green trees.

Friends, enemies, and strangers,
Each clasps the next one's hand:
They take turns calling changes.
I see in dreams the dancers.

Old men have grown to young men
And in the golden ring
Each man's a handsome king
Each lady is a queen.

I see in dreams the dancers
Build London Bridge again
When it had fallen down.
They are no longer strangers.
All, all of them are friends.

I watch the joyful dancers
As they move to and fro:
Death cannot touch them now.
They are no longer strangers.

When shall I join the dancers?

WORDS

Words, how they comfort,
how I hold them to me
as I held the pebbles
I collected as a child

going to sleep
holding them clasped
in my hand
tears on my cheek

or the necklace
of green and blue glass
that I loved and stroked.

I think
when I die
someone will find
a clutch of pebbled words
a peire of rhymes
under my pillow.

167

MAN AND MOON

How many moons are in the sky?
How many men are in the moon?
How many minds are in a man?
How many changes in a thought?
In any change, how many deaths?

Each day we know as many deaths
as there are valleys in the moon
or wandering meteors in the sky
that may be measured by a thought
or pictured by the camera mind
clicking behind the eyes of man.

As strange and variable is man
as mislaunched rocket in the sky
that cannot touch the spinning moon
but wanders from its course; his mind
is corpse-full of the minute deaths
of frivolous and changing thought.

Reason, the bright star of his thought,
is as inconstant as the moon
(so often scolded thus by man).
Clouds dim the radiance of his sky.
Rain, hail, pour down their icy deaths
on the frail blossoms of his mind.

And yet it is the inconstant mind,
darkened by all its many deaths,
that shines renewed in blossoming thought;
or, like a young space-travelling man,
that weightless walks the eerie sky
half way between the earth and moon,

it leaps and falls from earth to moon,
from moon to earth. Strange is the mind,
strange and far-seeing is the thought
of foolish, strange, inconstant man,
who leaps up from his million deaths
and is a meteor in the sky.

Yes, man is stranger than the moon.
His thought transcends his many deaths.
It is his mind that holds the sky.

THE GREEN GRASS GROWS ALL AROUND

I wonder there has been no population explosion
in the realms of the dead; there are so many of them:
so many tombs, from that of twice-dead Lazarus
to Prince Albert at Frogmore or the Unknown Soldier;
so many souls rustling down the autumns of time
dry Vallombrosan leaves; so many bodies
swathed in linen, dressed in toga or ruff,
or wearing (like my Aunt Grace at a picnic)
straw hats with shining
red wax cherries.

Where are they all? In far wastes of sky
(as my grandmother thought)
beyond the reach of space travellers,
or close by pressing around us
with rustlings and whisperings?

Do they talk to each other, the dead (living) souls,
Nero and Hitler, Socrates and Schweitzer,
St. Paul and the Queen of Sheba?
What do they find to say?
Do they speak in words? in code?
in a sort of shimmering
like new leaves in the spring?

Clustering, they await in groups
(perhaps) the Great Trump,
the explosion, the nuclear farewell which we dread
when the atoms of their reunited flesh may shine
in the pristine freshness of toga, ruff, straw hat
    with nodding cherries.

Supple as new trees, they will spring up
in the fresh ground,
the twice-turned
fragrant
ever-new earth
which the meek will inherit
and plough again with oxen
or the shining, sleek,
heel-kicking horses

while underground moulder
tractors, town halls, airports,
the Colosseum,
the Tower of Babel.

ELEGY FOR JEAN

Last night I thought of you,
and, half believing in ghosts, I seemed to see
you sitting in the chair beside me, leaning
a little forward, eager for argument.
We had been drinking tea, it seemed,
scalding and strong, six cups or so of it,
and talking of all the subjects under the sun;
and you, with your shrewd, plain, clever face lit up
with the joy of combat, waved an eager hand,
gesticulating to make clear your point.

I remember once we argued into the night
on immortality. Have you come back
to tell me that you've won the argument?
Not Plato or the four Evangelists
could so convince me as your death.
Others might die, but you, so vital,
with such a thirst for life that even being seasick
was a sort of joke, an experience to be savoured;
who were delighted with so many things—
fish and chips with beer, the tunes of organ grinders,
Eliot's cat poems, your landlady's husband's paintings,
zoos and railway stations and country walks—
I know you could not die.
                              I see you clumping into eternity
in your brown brogues, wearing your shabbiest skirt;
not beautiful, not dignified or graceful,
but always loved and loveable; stubborn and rude
but candid as a child, wholly yourself.

LINES TO JOHN BUNYAN

Say, Tinker John,
John Bunyan,
after all those trials
and the sloughs and bogs
and after the encounters with giants
and with fiends
fierce as highwaymen

were you able to rest
in delectable valleys?
were you not bored
with silver rivers
flowing past
clipped green trees,
with flowers laid out in just-so squares

and the cobbled golden streets
of the great City, the new

Hierusalem?

172

VICTORIA DAY, TORONTO

I sit this morning in a garden chair
under the trees beside the Museum
and watch the chinks of light between the leaves
or the people walking past on Bloor Street.
Outside the fence there is a great chestnut tree
with pyramids of blossom.
Inside, shrubs grow (cherry blossom?)
between the statues
which were carved for Chinese tombs
(the great bell, the delicate dancing girls, the dragon).
Within the squat building, death is present,
scary in mummies and fossilized skeletons,
wistful in pottery made by dead fingers,
harpsichords and spinets played by ghosts;
but here outdoors, I think, there is only life.

I think of hospitals,
the starched nurses
efficient
the white walls of pain.
And you are trapped
inside those walls
breathing disinfectant
closed in from flowering trees
and the people flowering on the city streets
while I, for now, am free.

I remember my mother died in May
and I drove to her funeral
down country roads
among the new leaves
and the apple blossoms.

If I could live to spring...
If I could live to summer...
Is that what she thought?

And she was buried on the old queen's birthday,
the queen who ruled
when she was a little girl
("If they don't give us a holiday
we'll all run away")

After the funeral walking in the woods
the children found wildflowers.

Now, all these years later,
I am afraid again
of the death behind the blossom.

The day grows hotter.
The pompous overfed pigeons
rummage among the garbage.
A squirrel at a painted picnic table
gnaws at an apple core.

Nothing moves quickly enough
I think until a small dog runs
across the lawn
and squirrels, pigeons, even people
scatter in flight.

I walk back down the street
to my narrow coffin-shaped hotel room.
On the walls I count
the small stylized daisies.

ELEGY NOT WRITTEN

I would like to write you a poem
because you would have liked me to write a poem.
You were sentimental about such things.

But I can't write.
I don't believe you are dead.
And if you are
who any longer will read my poems?

175

LIFE IS A FLOWING

Life you said
is a flowing
contains death

Yesterday
I heard you had died.
A great stone
blocks the current.
Only the smallest trickle
of living
water
can pass

though it boils up
angrily
against the stone.

Outside my window
the leaves ripple in the wind.
Midsummer
is over.

From now on
the days will grow
shorter.

Life is a flowing
Life is

death is
life
flowing

SYNCHRONICITY

Just before midnight you died.
Here it was nine o'clock:
the pink flush of sunset
suffused the prairie sky.
Hot weather both here and there.
That morning, here, a thunderstorm
woke me. I was restless all day,
could not settle to anything.
In the evening, I
sorted my books, sat turning pages,
read a poem of Auden's
about loneliness,
stepped out once
onto the balcony,
but my old fear of heights
returned on me
and I came in.

When the clock struck nine,
I looked out and saw
the pink flood of the clouds
against pale blue,
the hackneyed, beautiful sunset

and I wondered about you
and wondered if your mind moved freely
and if my mind could touch it

slept better that night
than I had for some time past
but was not surprised
in the morning
by the ring of the telephone.

DANCE OF DEATH

I dreamed of the dance of death,
the great skeleton dancing with the guests
and showing all the ways of dying.
"Pick your poison," he seemed to say:
"old age, strokes, heart attacks,
suicide, murder,
drowning, strangulation by smog,
the creeping cancer.
What death is most truly You?"

Then I left him and entered a church—
or was it a wax museum?—
where there were rows of rooms
brightly lit to celebrate
births and marriages
and filled with images
of nativity scenes
or waxen bridal couples

but the biggest room
belonged to death.
I stood outside a thin
semi-transparent curtain
wondering if I should go in
to light candles and pray for my dead.

The curtain slid back
only a fraction
to let me through,
but I was afraid
and hesitated.
"If I go in," I asked,
"am I sure to come out?"
and I could imagine vaults stretching
a long way into the shadows
and the bodies of unknown sleepers
far below.

"It's the least I can do for them,"
I said.
"This is no Chamber of Horrors."
I started forward,
but I was too late.
The curtain closed while I was watching,
and, flimsy though it looked,
I could not budge it.

All night I bruised myself
against its folds.

Shall I not now
see past the curtain?
Or is there nothing to see?

179

Come back, Master Death,
old barefaced jester.
I refuse to be intimidated
by your rattling bones.
Surely in the sockets of your eyes
there are flowers growing.
Surely (though I tremble)
you cannot change
something to nothing.

I see them walking
hand in hand
by the shores of a blue bay.
They are climbing the rocks
talking,
one helping the other,
and sooner or later
one of them will see me

one of them will wave

180

LABOUR DAY AGAIN

It is Labour Day again.
Autumn is early this year.
I sit once more on a bench
by the Saskatchewan River
and see that the leaves are already turning,
rowans are red, nasturtiums orange.
I wear a coat and shiver.

Again I say to myself
(as I said before)
I still miss you,
but this time the space between us
is wider than prairie
or even than lack of understanding.
The space is death.

Yet, sitting here,
I have seldom felt more alive,
more conscious
of the atoms of my flesh dancing,
knowing that life is a fire
that I burn like leaves
in the bonfire of time.

What looks solid and frozen—
ice, rocks, bodies—
really burns or flows.
Each melts into all.

I have not time for grief.
I too, I too,
I say,
as the clouds shift
and all the rivers flow

V: Renewal

THERE IS TIME

to begin again
to write new poems for the new land
to start life over
to find a new lover
or a dozen lovers
to follow where the hands beckon
to create
and uncreate.

I am not young
but neither am I old.
I have twenty years
more maybe
before earth takes me
breaks me again
and makes me snail or flower.

"Death is inevitable,"
my old lover said.
"Giving in isn't."
And I believe
though perhaps he did not believe
himself.

All I have done
seems sometimes waste
scribble on sand
but always
it can be done over.

Not permanence
not the eternal footprints in the sands of
etcetera
but the feel of
writing in sand with a broken stick
rough bark under the fingers
or the feel of toes in wet sand

There is time
yet
I can start again

there is time

183

ON READING ANOTHER POET

I think we are being given the same messages
that oracles are speaking in our dreams
warning admonition code
syllables of unknown meaning.

We are not in competition.
If I say the same thing
it is not because I copy
but because the voice says so.

Maybe there will be hundreds of us
like choric echoes.
It will not matter
that the words repeat themselves

so long as what is said
rises like the tide in all our separate waves
and beats upon and shapes the dreaming shore.

184

UNITY

"All poets are one poet,"
Pat Page says.
"If they are
he's a schizophrenic,"
I reply, thinking
of feuds, divisions,
differences in metrical theory,
and mountains not on speaking terms
with prairie.

Nevertheless
we may both be right.

FOR THE MALE IN SEARCH OF THE
WHITE GODDESS

Containing both, being neither
untouched virgin
nor harlot in a red dress

I am myself, individual,

never "just like a woman"
though certainly female.

If you want to call me a goddess
I don't object
though nobody else has called me one

(not a bitch-goddess either)

I know I'm human
unfashionable
unadorned
am only beautiful without clothes

never wore eye makeup
never used a deodorant
but I like perfume.

I do not object
within reason
to male swaggering
(don't necessarily expect it either)

will promise not to say
"Isn't that just like a man?"

When I was growing up
it was my father who wept
at the sad bits in movies.
My mother never cried.

As for me, I take after
both my parents.

186

ANTI-LOVE POEMS

I

No, I don't love you
in spite of what I say
in the ecstasy of the act.

Don't preen,
Don't worry.
It isn't
the way you think it is.
(How do I know
what you think?)

Why do I feel guilty
that I am sometimes bored?
That I compare your
hands with other hands?
That I remember other faces
better than I remember yours?

It's not your fault.
Love is never deserved,
is mostly imagination anyway.

It's only fretfulness that I complain
you are not warmer, gayer, tenderer,
don't have brown eyes,
have the same faults I have.

Now that I have opened
all my doors to you,
could I close them again?
Would I really love you, maybe,
only if you went away?

Is unrequited love
what I have always wanted
because it takes less time
than the other kind?

2

Yet I do sympathize,
try to understand
the scared small boy in a bleak boarding school
with all those dotty and perverse masters

boy who killed a bird once
not knowing why

(the story frightened me,
   bird-woman that I am,
   perched
   assailable
   always scared
   of having my wings maimed)

but you wanted then to be punished,
maybe still do.

I understand better
the time you stole
the model sailing ship
(because once I stole
   a beaded purse from my cousin's box of popcorn
   and Grandmother said
   I would end up in prison
   eating bread and water)

and the way you idolized
your reckless charmer
disreputable father
who went from job to job
and wife to wife

and that sailor
who dared you to swim
in the shark-infested sea
(you felt he would scorn you forever
   because you could not do it)

always punishing yourself
by failing,
not daring,
not wanting to hope too much.

I wonder, do you see me
as bird, or ship, or shark?

189

RENEWAL

Expecting only consolation,
astonished to tears
by ecstasy

I have no words
except the child babble of lovers
repeating "love love love"
repeating your name

as you press within me
as I feel you plummeting
                            space traveller
                            deep sea diver

                                        into my live centre

and hold you rocking rocking
on all my waves.

Returned,
you tell me
it was like falling
down slopes of
moist iris petals.

And I marvel
as though I were young
as I never was
and rise ageless
from the seaweed-scented fishfoam
of our joined bodies.

CLIMATE

You say you imagine you are on a beach
in the hot white sand by a blue bay
and there are children chattering in the distance
and an ice-cream vendor with his cart
calling his wares
and you are lying in the sun
getting the most marvellous tan

but I am satisfied to be right here
now
surrounded by friendly furniture,
lying between the sheets with you,
the lights off,
only my Christmas candle burning,
somebody singing on television.

It's twenty below outside—
or is it thirty?—
but in this room
together
it's quite warm enough
for me.

191

FRAGMENTS

Showing each other these fragments
of our pasts—poems, snapshots
of our youthful faces
innocent and open,
or other faces lost,
estranged, dead, distant

places where we lived
(those foreign trees—
jacarandas?—
with pink-purple blooms
under whose branches
the doves coo-roo:
I see them against
all my grey birches
and farmyard fowl)

we trade our selves
and all our years,
pride, loss, failure
traced on silvered paper.

Strange to have come
from those diverse origins
our separate paths
to reach this quiet room
in the land's centre

this fragmentary peace
our hands touching

sun and moon colliding

LATE VALENTINE

Willing, finally,
to risk caring for you,
to see you as yourself,
not those others,
not father, brother,
or lover lost or invented,
but you yourself;

belatedly, grudgingly,
mind follows body,
peels off its protection,
takes you within me.

And now I can relax.
It does not matter
if the union
is something less than ecstatic.
I accept this touch,
this sometimes hurting,
my inadequacy or yours.
Your embrace
is real. It is no fiction.
It is more important than poetry.

I no longer say "I love you"
because I nearly do.

ON BECOMING AN ANCESTOR

Too late in life
for children, the building
of flesh and bone
out of flesh and bone,
all that blood and guts
other women talk of.

By chance or intention
whatever touching
of body or mind
came too late.

Not my fault, it seems to me,
I would have liked
I think

Or maybe I was scared.
Many things scared me.

Does it matter?
Flesh becomes
the green blood of grass.
Poems disintegrate
to their original syllables.

There is no avoiding
the process of transformation,
of becoming
a sort of ancestor,
like the lovers in old songs
from whose buried mouths
grew briars and roses.

My fears were unnecessary
but after all did not change
the end result
which (whether I fear or hope)
is not an end

TAROT

Telling my own fortune with the cards
(bad luck, I suppose)
I am half amused, half frightened
by this pack
of archetypal symbols
which mean for tonight
what I design them to mean.

The charioteer drives his two mismatched horses.
There again are the lovers
bathed as usual in illusory light
with Eros poised above them.
Emotions: the high tower, meaning (maybe)
divorce, separation, anger.

My future is the High Priestess,
my past the Empress,
maternal Juno, strong woman,
procreative.
For others (can I believe this?)
I am the Star,
naked lady with a watering-can
bending over her flowers,
an Eve or Kore.
A good card. Good luck.

No Death this time,
but there is the Devil,
Disaster ending all

(can be avoided.
After all, he is only made of cardboard.)

My own card is Magician
(Prospero? Faust? Gypsy woman?)
I wear special robes
and hold my wand in my hand.
I can build an island
of my own.
I can let the world in
or keep it out.
The island is mine
   (though may survive me
   and belong then to others).

My cards are given me,
but I can play them to suit myself.
I can prevent the horses of the charioteer
from throwing him to the ground.

I can be Empress one day
and High Priestess the next.
I can confront Devil with Star
and make her win
(it is done all the time in fairy tales).

But what can I do with the tower?
I live in it
and am afraid of falling.

Dreamed the other night
of climbing a rope ladder
fainting at every step
dizzy with fright.
Once almost
I lost my footing,
but hands reached out
and held my hand,
and someone behind me
unseen
supported me from falling.
My foot only barely
reached the rung,
but I survived.

I would like to live in a house,
a cottage even,
but a tower is what I am given.
There is no use quarrelling with the cards,
and besides I have a view
that would delight any magician.

Nevertheless, if my cards change,
some time again
I may think of moving.

ELIZABETH BREWSTER was born in New Brunswick, but since 1972 has lived in Saskatoon, where she is now a Professor Emeritus at the University of Saskatchewan. She has published five books of fiction, two volumes of autobiography and twenty collections of poetry. *Footnotes to the Book of Job* was shortlisted for the Governor General's Award, and her most recent collection, *Jacob's Dream*, received the Saskatchewan Book Award for Poetry in 2003. She has been awarded an honorary doctorate by the University of New Brunswick, the E.J. Pratt Award and the President's Medal, as well as the Saskatchewan Lifetime Achievement Award. In the last three years she has turned eighty years of age, converted to Judaism and become a member of the Order of Canada.